DATE DUE		

Yankee Doodle and the Redcoats

SOLDIERING IN THE REVOLUTIONARY WAR

SUSAN PROVOST BELLER ✳ *With illustrations by* Larry Day

TWENTY-FIRST CENTURY BOOKS
Brookfield, Connecticut

For Susan Jackson,
a loyal fan
and
an enduring friend
　　　　　　—S. P. B.

For Amy Cawley, J. Perkins,
Al Potyen, and Dave Nordin,
members of the Northwest
Territory Alliance and the First
Division Museum at Cantigny.
　　　　　　—L. D.

Library of Congress Cataloging-in-Publication Data
Beller, Susan Provost, 1949-
Yankee Doodle and the Redcoats : soldiering in the Revolutionary War /
Susan Provost Beller ; with illustrations by Larry Day.
p. cm.
Summary: Using excerpts from diaries, letters, newspaper articles, and
other primary sources, tells of the everyday lives of the soldiers who
fought the Revolutionary War, for both the British and for the colonies.
Includes bibliographical references and index.
ISBN 0-7613-2612-X
1. United States. Continental Army—Military life—Juvenile
literature. 2. Great Britain. Army—Military life—History—18th
century—Juvenile literature. 3. United States—History—Revolution,
1775-1783—Personal narratives—Juvenile literature. 4. United
States—History—Revolution, 1775-1783—Social aspects—Juvenile
literature. 5. Soldiers—United States—Social conditions—18th
century—Juvenile literature. 6. Soldiers—United States—Biography—
Juvenile literature. [1. United States. Continental Army—Military life.
2. Great Britain. Army—Military life—History—18th century. 3. United
States—History—Revolution, 1775-1783—Personal narratives. 4. United
States—History—Revolution, 1775-1783—Social aspects. 5. Soldiers.]
I. Day, Larry, 1956- ill. II. Title.
E259 .B45 2003   973.3—dc21   2002001057

Photographs courtesy of Library of Congress: pp. 2, 10, 35,
57, 61, 69; North Wind Picture Archives: pp. 15, 19, 23,
26, 32, 49, 53, 64, 80, 85; National Archives: pp. 20, 27, 45,
79; The Granger Collection, New York: p. 75
Map by Joe LeMonnier

Published by Twenty-First Century Books
A Division of The Millbrook Press, Inc.
2 Old New Milford Road
Brookfield, Connecticut 06804
www.millbrookpress.com

Contents

PROLOGUE

"It was utterly out of my power to refuse this appointment without exposing my Character to such censure as would have reflected dishonour upon myself,"[1] wrote George Washington to his wife about his decision to accept the appointment of commander in chief of the Continental army.

Marie-Joseph-Paul-Yves-Roch-Gilbert du Motier, known to Americans by his title, the Marquis de Lafayette, also joined the fight on the side of the colonies. He wrote: "The moment I heard of America I loved her; the moment I knew she was fighting for liberty I burnt with a desire of bleeding for her."[2]

Hessian General Friedrich von Riedesel, fighting on the side of the British, wrote to his wife: "Never have I suffered more than upon my departure this morning. My heart was broken . . . . But, my darling, God has placed me in my present calling, and I must follow it. Duty and honor force me to this decision."[3]

British soldier Thomas Anburey wrote at the end of one battle: "We have gained little more by our victory than honour."[4]

Loyalist Major Thomas Barclay wrote of those in the colonies remaining true to the king as wanting to "preserve their principles of honor and integrity, of openness and sincerity."[5]

What do these five gentlemen have in common? It is the fact that they were fighting in the American Revolution. Although two were allied in the fight for independence and three were their enemies, the common theme is honor. It is a theme often repeated among the famous and not so famous who found themselves soldiers in this struggle for independence.

When we speak of the Founding Fathers, the great men who were responsible for helping form the

United States, we usually talk of Thomas Jefferson, the writer of the Declaration of Independence, and famous Patriots such as Benjamin Franklin and John Adams, who served as ambassadors for the new nation during the Revolutionary War. We usually include George Washington, of course, in recognition of his role as commander in chief of the Continental army. Beyond that, we rarely take the time to consider the many other individuals who, by working together, made it possible for this country to actually exist. And we definitely fail to account for those who suffered defeat.

But the American Revolution—this war of honor—was not won by Thomas Jefferson or the American ambassadors. This revolution was won by all those Patriot soldiers, from the minutemen and the Green Mountain Boys to those who became regular soldiers in the Continental army. It was the everyday militiamen and others who left their homes and fought against what was at that time the best army in the world, who won independence for the American colonies. It was also won by those allies like the French officers Rochambeau and Lafayette, the German drillmaster von Steuben, and the Polish engineer Thaddeus Kosciusko.

It was also a war about honor for those who lost the Revolution. Whether the Loyalist troops who remained in support of the king when their fellow colonists rebelled, the troops from Hesse and other provinces in Germany, who fought in a land where they did not even understand the language, or the British troops called Redcoats, or lobsterbacks because of their red uniforms, who suffered terrible humiliation at the hands of these untrained colonial soldiers—each group played a part in the beginning of this country that we are so proud of today.

Because the American Revolution happened so long ago, it is sometimes hard to imagine what life must have been like for soldiers on both sides—those who fought for the ideal of liberty and those who fought to defend their belief in the divine right of the king. Although they fought for different sides and different causes, these soldiers had much in common. In this book, those soldiers from so long ago tell us the story of what they did and how they won or lost the war that made us a nation.

A Word About Words

Rebels, Patriots, Yankee Doodles, Whigs, Americans? Hessians, Germans? Loyalists, Royalists, Tories? Redcoats, lobsterbacks, bloodybacks? What we call the participants in the American Revolution could be a book in itself, and the author has to

American soldier

make a decision on which labels to use.

The Americans who supported the cause of independence called themselves Americans. So did those who remained loyal to the king! In this book you will find those who supported independence referred to as Patriots. Those who remained in support of the king are called Loyalists. A taunting song called all the "rebels" Yankee Doodle. The Patriots throughout the colonies took the song as their own in defiance of the image it gave of them. Using the term *Yankee Doodle* in the title of this book commemorates the defiant attitude of those who fought for independence.

The British soldiers are commonly called Redcoats, although memoirs written at the time often call them more negative things. The British

officer in charge at the Boston Massacre, Captain Thomas Preston, said in his trial that the "mob" called them "bloody backs" and "lobster scoundrels."

Fighting alongside the British were the soldiers known as Hessians. They came from several independent states that a long time after the Revolutionary War united to become Germany. Some historians call these soldiers Germans to reflect that they were not just from the province of Hesse. Here you will find them called Hessians.

Whatever we call its characters, this is a story about honor and the way all of these people fought to defend their beliefs. The labels matter not. What matters is the devotion these people brought to the effort.

British soldier

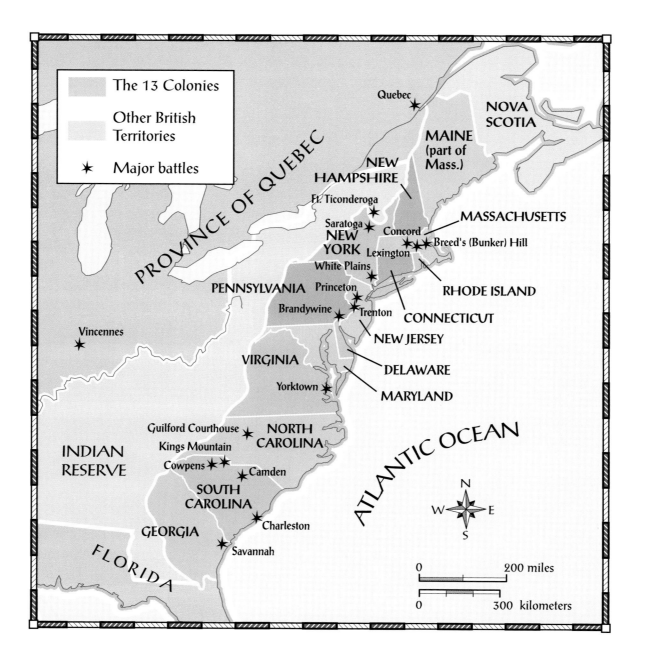

The 13 Colonies

Other British Territories

★ Major battles

Quebec ★

NOVA SCOTIA

PROVINCE OF QUEBEC

MAINE (part of Mass.)

NEW HAMPSHIRE

Ft. Ticonderoga

MASSACHUSETTS

Saratoga ★

NEW YORK

Concord ★

★ Breed's (Bunker) Hill

Lexington

White Plains ★

PENNSYLVANIA

Princeton ★

Brandywine ★ ★ Trenton

RHODE ISLAND

CONNECTICUT

NEW JERSEY

DELAWARE

MARYLAND

Vincennes ★

VIRGINIA

Yorktown ★

Guilford Courthouse ★

NORTH CAROLINA

INDIAN RESERVE

Kings Mountain

Cowpens ★ ★

Camden ★

SOUTH CAROLINA

ATLANTIC OCEAN

GEORGIA

★ Charleston

Savannah ★

FLORIDA

N
W   E
S

0   200 miles

0   300 kilometers

CHAPTER ONE

Patriot or Loyalist?

Imagine for a moment that you are a colonist living in America in the 1770s. Your mother country, Great Britain, has lately been increasing the amount of taxes you must pay on goods that you need every day. You are angry about this. No one is allowing you or your representatives who serve in the colonial legislatures any voice in this process.

The king, through his Parliament, claims that the reason for these new taxes is that the mother country has incurred a great deal of debt fighting to protect you in the war that those in England call the Seven Years' War, the one you call the French and Indian War. But you feel that you have already paid your debt for that war. After all, you defended yourself, fighting in the colonial militia alongside the British soldiers. It was your land and your homes that suffered in the attacks by the French soldiers and their Indian allies.

Perhaps you find yourself angry enough to think that someone must do something to stop Parliament and King George III from interfering in the colonies. But is that something a revolution? Does that something have to be a war for independence?

That was the decision that faced the colonists as the conflict with Great Britain escalated in the 1760s and 1770s. The colonists were angry at the number of taxes they were forced to pay to the crown, especially since they had no one representing their interests in deciding what taxes would be levied. The cry of "No taxation without representation" was universal in the colonies.

The differences of opinion that arose among the colonists were not over whether Great Britain and King George III were wrong—that they could agree on. What caused division among them was the issue of how strongly they could (or should) respond to

The actions of King George III of Great Britain and his Parliament pushed American colonists first to protest, then to resistance, and finally to revolution.

Parliament's refusal to address their grievances. How could they best demand the rights to which all Englishmen were entitled, rights they felt they still had as colonists?

A motion in the Virginia House of Burgesses stated on May 29, 1765: "The first adventurers and settlers of this his Majesty's colony and dominion of Virginia, brought with them . . . all the privileges and immunities that have at any time been held, enjoyed, and possessed by the people of Great Britain."[1] It is important to remember that the colonists truly felt that they were asking for only what they already were entitled to as British citizens.

There were those colonists whose anger at Britain led them to speak of independence very early in the process. They were a very small group. Even by the time war broke out, the Patriots represented only about one third of the colonial population. There were good reasons for this group remaining small.

Reasonable people looked at the situation this way: Great Britain was the major colonial power at the time. It had just defeated France, the second-largest colonial power, in a bitter seven-year struggle, which had cost France its colony in Canada. Great Britain had the world's finest navy. Great Britain also had the world's finest army, with highly trained and disciplined soldiers. And Great Britain had sufficient resources to sustain a long-term war, if necessary. If the British government had been able to defeat the French (their closest equals in military and financial power), defeating their colonists would be quite a simple task.

Reasonable colonists looked at the possibility of revolution and were horrified. They saw near-certain defeat and then a mother country that would punish them harshly for their defiance. The Loyalists (also called Royalists or Tories) viewed defiance of the king as a certain disaster for them personally and for the rights of future generations of colonists. These Loyalists made up another third of the colonial population. The last third was made up of those who remained fairly neutral or were opposed to war for religious reasons, like the Quakers.

The discussion of these critical issues rapidly led to bitter division among the colonists. The supporters of independence came to see the other side as disloyal. What had been a civil conversation and debate became more forceful. Stories abound of loyal subjects of the king being tarred and feathered or having their property destroyed by their angry neighbors. Wrote one Loyalist: "Though I really had no views nor wishes but such as I believed to be for the true interest of the country, all the forward and noisy patriots, both in the Assembly and out of it, agreed to consider me as an obnoxious person."[2]

The discussion even caused problems for individual families. One of the earliest supporters of independence, Benjamin Franklin of Philadelphia, saw his son, William, the colonial governor of the New Jersey colony, remain an avid supporter of the king. The country's dispute would divide them forever.

With such strong Loyalist support in the colonies and with the support for separation still relatively small, compromise on the part of Parliament and the king could easily have led to a peaceful solution to the disagreement. However, the British leaders stubbornly ignored the complaints of the colonists. Their refusal to even discuss the merits of the dispute and their continued passage of legislation that further angered the colonies gave the Patriots all the ammunition they needed to finally reach a decision for independence.

On February 20, 1775, the Provincial Congress of Massachusetts passed a resolution advising the citizens of the colony to prepare for coming war: "Most earnestly recommended to the militia in general, as well as the detached part of it in minutemen, that they spare neither time, pains, nor expenses . . . in perfecting themselves forthwith in military discipline . . . that they encourage such persons as are skilled in the manufactory of fire-arms and bayonets, diligently to apply themselves there for supplying such of the inhabitants as shall be deficient."[3] The actual Declaration of Independence would not come until July 4, 1776. But the first fighting was only two months away. Yankee Doodle would meet the Redcoats at Lexington, Massachusetts, on April 19, 1775.

*Stories abound of loyal subjects of
the king being tarred and feathered or
having their property destroyed by
their angry neighbors.*

In response, the Second Continental Congress convened. Unlike the first, which simply sent a list of grievances to the king in 1774, this one appointed a military commander. In July they sent one last petition to the king, asking that all military action stop until their issues could be discussed. When the king rejected this so-called Olive Branch Petition, the Second Continental Congress voted for independence and formed a government to fight a war. When a peace treaty was finally signed on September 3, 1783, the impossible had happened—Great Britain had lost and the United States of America had successfully achieved independence from the mightiest colonial power on Earth.

How did this happen? As new American Eliza Wilkinson, a young South Carolina girl whose family had to evacuate their home several times in the course of the war, reminisced: "When [the British] embarked for America, they were sure of success; for they expected no opposition from a people so little skilled in arms; and who had no experience in the art of war; but to their cost they found, that those who have a true sense of their rights and liberties, will 'conquer difficulties by daring to oppose them.' "[4]

CHAPTER TWO

The Soldiers From Home— the Patriots and Loyalists

On April 4, 1775, *Holt's Journal*, a colonial newspaper, reported on a letter from London telling of "a royal proclamation, declaring the inhabitants of Massachusetts Bay . . . actual rebels, with a blank commission to try and execute such of them as he [British General Thomas Gage] can get hold of."[1]

With the arrival of Gage's orders from London, the long-expected conflict was imminent. Militiamen, groups of soldiers organized by town, had been drilling for some time. The minutemen, trained to respond instantly, were ready for whatever action the British would take. On April 19, 1775, British troops left Boston in search of rebels that they knew were hiding in the countryside west of Boston. The British planned to capture these rebels along with their supplies and gunpowder. The

Patriots had been warned and knew they were coming. Later that morning a member of the Committee of Safety of Watertown, Massachusetts, sent messenger Israel Bissell to spread the alarming story to the rest of the colonies. It was important that other militias know not just of the morning's attack but that "we find another Brigade are now upon their march from Boston supposed to be about 1,000."[2] It appeared that the British were not planning this to be just a onetime attack.

As word of this action at Lexington and Concord spread through the colonies, Patriots rushed to organize themselves for battle. Young Elkanah Watson had recently joined a cadet company in the Rhode Island colony. When news of the attack reached Providence that afternoon, he wrote: "Our five companies flew to arms. The whole population was convulsed with the most vehement excitement. We were unprovided with cartridges; and were compelled to defer our march until morning. I spent most of that agitated night, with many of our company, in running bullets and preparing ammunition. We mustered early the next morning, and marched for the scene of action."[3]

The next several months were a period of organization as the colonists transformed from a group of unorganized militias to the Continental army. The most important decision to be made was a political one. Who should lead the army? The Continental Congress selected a Virginia planter, George Washington. His selection tied together the colonies,

The minutemen, as they were known, were a militia trained to respond instantly to a crisis. They heeded the call as British soldiers marched on Lexington, Massachusetts.

keeping this from breaking down into a fight between the Massachusetts Bay Colony and the government of King George III. The delegates to the Continental Congress were heeding the words of member Benjamin Franklin: "We must all hang together, or assuredly we shall all hang separately."[4]

With a formal Declaration of Independence still more than a year away, keeping the colonies working together was a demanding job for the president of the Continental Congress, John Hancock. All of the leaders were aware of the death sentence that awaited them for treason if this rebellion was unsuccessful. The man appointed to be commander in chief would be especially vulnerable. Washington had military experience, fighting with the British in the French and Indian War. And he was a pleasant man, easily able to work with others—an important quality in trying to organize an army from all of the very independent colonies.

George Washington wrote to his wife on June 18, 1775, telling her of his appointment to the post. "You may believe me, my dear . . . when I assure you, in the most solemn manner, that so far from seeking this appointment I have used every endeavor in my power to avoid it . . . from a consciousness of its being a trust too great for my Capacity." He wrote: "I was apprehensive that I could not avoid this appointment" and that he accepted it now because it was a matter of honor, and to refuse it "would have lessened me considerably in my own esteem."[5] His decision to defend his country and the rights that he believed were being violated was mirrored in thousands of other Americans now facing the choice of active rebellion against the crown.

The formal instructions given to George Washington by the Continental Congress assigned him a broad range of duties. They make the situation sound much more organized than it really was. "You are to Repair with all Expedition to the Colony of Massachusetts Bay, & Take Charge of the Army of the United Colonies. . . . You are to make a Return to us as soon as possible of all Forces which you shall have under your Command, together with their Military Stores and Provisions."[6]

In fact, there was as yet no army for Washington to command. The militia had indeed responded quite well to the emergency. But militiamen were only part-time soldiers, drilling on their town greens. They were perhaps as far from being professional soldiers as it was possible to be. They were independent and unused to following orders. Their officers tended to be men who would not easily give up the authority over "their" regiments to an outsider. More important, they were men who had other commit-

General George Washington was faced with building an army from the ground up.

ments in their lives. They would serve in an immediate crisis, but they were not necessarily available to serve for the course of a long war.

General George Washington was faced with building an army from the ground up. He would be plagued throughout the war with insufficient numbers of well-trained fighting men. Many times he would have access to many different groups of militia, defending the area where they lived. But these men would not have the training needed to fight against the disciplined British Redcoats and the Hessians they employed. These militias, perhaps unfairly, would earn a reputation for firing a few times in battle and then leaving the field.

Washington would try throughout the war to fashion an effective fighting force made up of smaller numbers of more trained soldiers integrated with the militias to give him the force he needed to fight. It was a difficult task for a commander, and achieving it may have been his greatest success as a military leader.

The militias also had a bad effect at times on the overall morale of the army. One officer of the Continental army, Lieutenant Benjamin Gilbert, wrote home of his frustration with having to train recruits whose stay in the army was for only a short period of time, calling them "undissiplined" [sic] and complaining that their fighting made even the "bravest officer . . . lose his honour."[7] Another officer noted that "it has been found, by sad experience, that but little dependence can be placed on an army of militia, and those whose term of service is so short that they are almost continually fluctuating from camp to their farms."[8]

What could a soldier who joined the Continental army expect to receive for his services beyond the long-term prospect of victory and independence? The Orderly Book kept at Fort Ticonderoga in New York records the offer being made for enlistment in October 1776:

The Honl Congress of the United States have for the Reward and Encouragement of every Non Commission'd Officer and Soldier who shall engage to serve during the War further resolve to give (over and above the Bounty of Twenty Dollars) to each Man Annually one Complete Suit of Cloathing which for the Present Year is to consist of Two Linnen Hunting Shirts, Two Pear of Stockings, Two Pear of Shoes, Two Pear of Over Alls, a Leathren or Woolen Jackett with Sleeves, One Pear of Breeches and One Leather Cap or Hatt, amounting in the Whole to the Value of 20 Dollars or that Sum to be paid to each Soldier who shall procure these Articles for himself. . . . This Noble Bounty of 20 Dollars & One Hundred Acres of Land at the End of the War is such an Ample and Generous Gratuity.[9]

It was indeed a generous offer for the times. As we shall later see, the problem was in actually being able to provide what was barely needed, let alone such generous benefits.

Militiamen were drawn from all able-bodied men between the ages of sixteen and sixty living in a community. The Continental army itself had (as is true in most wars) a younger population, since it is usually the young who can be away from home for the time required, and who can better withstand the rigors of training and life as a soldier. Each state was

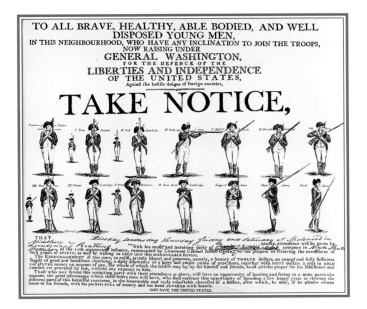

TO ALL BRAVE, HEALTHY, ABLE BODIED, AND WELL
DISPOSED YOUNG MEN,
IN THIS NEIGHBOURHOOD, WHO HAVE ANY INCLINATION TO JOIN THE TROOPS,
NOW RAISING UNDER
GENERAL WASHINGTON,
FOR THE DEFENCE OF THE
LIBERTIES AND INDEPENDENCE
OF THE UNITED STATES,
Against the hostile designs of foreign enemies,

TAKE NOTICE,

As this recruiting poster indicates, young men were needed to fill the ranks of the newly forming Continental army.

responsible for providing a certain number of soldiers for the Continental army.

As we can see in the Ticonderoga Orderly Book, soldiers were offered bounties (money paid for signing up), uniforms, and land grants. They also received a monthly pay of about six to seven dollars. The problem with this system is that the states themselves were responsible for providing the sol-

diers and their equipment. General Washington found himself spending most of his time writing letters requesting that the states actually provide their agreed upon numbers of soldiers and supplies. When the soldiers and their supplies did not arrive as promised, he could only complain to John Hancock and the Continental Congress, hoping that the congress could elicit a better response.

Some of the soldiers were women, who were hired for camp chores. Some actually qualified for pensions after the war for their services. Wives and children also sometimes accompanied their soldiers with the army, which created problems for the commanders. Family members required provisions that were already scarce and sometimes got in the way of the army as it was marching. However many problems might be caused by their presence, sometimes the soldiers' wives could be lifesavers.

Such a lifesaver was the famous "Molly Pitcher," who earned her name at the Battle of Monmouth. Mary Ludwig Hays was the wife of a Pennsylvania soldier, William Hays, who was a gunner in an artillery battery. She traveled with her husband throughout his seven years of service in the Revolutionary War. She helped with the sick and wounded after battle, but she also participated during battle, carrying buckets (or pitchers) of water for the artillerymen to use to clean out the cannons

Margaret Ludwig Hays went down in history as the heroic "Molly Pitcher" after she served on the battlefield and later took command of her fallen husband's cannon.

between firing each round. During the New Jersey campaign, her husband was wounded and she stepped forward and continued his chores as a gunner for the remainder of the battle.

Margaret Corbin assisted her husband in his artillery post also. When he was killed at the Battle of Fort Washington, she continued in the cannon crew "until her own body was torn with grapeshot. She was maimed for life and permanently lost the use of one arm."[10] In 1779 the Continental Congress formally recognized her actions and awarded her a pension for the rest of her life.

At least one other woman served in the war as an actual enlisted soldier. Deborah Sampson enlisted under the name Robert Shurtleff and served as a soldier in the 4th Massachusetts Regiment. Her biographer, Herman Mann, included in his book about her the letter she wrote to her mother explaining her decision to join up and telling her, "Be not too much troubled, therefore, about my present or future engagements; as I will endeavor to make that prudence and virtue my model, for which, I own, I am much indebted to those, who took charge of my youth."[11] Apparently she was not prudent enough, since she was finally injured in battle and her identity found out. She did receive a pension for her military service.

Two other groups of soldiers are deserving of special mention for their service in the Revolutionary War. The first are the free blacks who enlisted to fight for the cause of independence. The first man to die in the pre–Revolutionary War struggle with Britain, Crispus Attucks, was black. He was one of the five colonists to die in the famous Boston Massacre that so inflamed the Patriots.

Several of the minutemen in the first battle of the war, at Lexington and Concord in April 1775, were also black. In the fighting at the Battle of Bunker Hill, historians estimate that there were about twenty black American soldiers. It should be noted that not all of the black soldiers fought for the Patriot cause. John Murray, Lord Dunmore, the royal governor of Virginia, organized a group of black soldiers into what he called his "Ethiopian Regiment" to fight with the Loyalists to defend the king. Dunmore promised them their freedom in return for their military service.

Freedom was also the promise made to the five thousand or so black soldiers who served in the fight for independence. There were eventually three units of black soldiers who served with the Continental army during the war. But not all of the blacks who fought did so to earn their freedom.

In the South, plantation owners would often send their slaves off to fight, simply as another chore for them to do. One slave who asked permission to enlist was James, owned by William Armistead of New Kent County, Virginia. He served as a double agent in British general Charles Cornwallis's camp, providing information for the Marquis de Lafayette that helped Lafayette prepare for battle with the British. After the war, Lafayette said of James: "His intelligences from the enemy's camp were industriously collected and more faithfully delivered. He perfectly acquitted himself . . . and appears to me entitled to every reward his situation can admit of."[12] His reward turned out to be his freedom when the Virginia General Assembly emancipated him in 1786. James chose a last name for himself—Lafayette.

Another group of people whose actions in the Revolutionary War deserve separate comment is the native peoples. As the war began, the Continental

Congress's greatest interest in Native Americans was to ensure that they remained neutral in the fight. Americans were aware that the native peoples had fought as British allies during the French and Indian War, and would probably respond favorably if asked to fight with the British again.

Seneca tribal leader, Thaonawyutha, known as Governor Blacksnake, recorded the message received by the tribes from the Continental Congress: "This is a family quarrel Between us and old England, you Indians, are not concerned in it, we Don't wish you to take up the hatchet [against] the King's troops, we Desire you to Remain at home, and not Join Either Side."[13] This "family quarrel" rapidly got out of hand, and the tribes became as divided in their loyalties as the colonists.

One historian describes what happened as an "American civil war . . . whites killed Indians, Indians killed whites, Indians killed Indians, and whites killed whites in guerrilla warfare."[14]

It is generally thought that more Native Americans fought with the British than against them since the greatest concern of many natives was the expansion of the colonists into native territories, which they rightly feared. Many historians feel that one of the reasons for the later discrimination against the native peoples was that most of them (or so it

was remembered) did support the British cause in the American Revolution. Whatever is true, this fight for freedom was not about freedom and equality for the native peoples.

Not all of the soldiers in this conflict who came from this side of the ocean were fighting for independence. Loyalist or Tory sentiment was most common in the middle and southern colonies. It is no surprise that these areas drew the largest number of soldiers for Loyalist regiments. Historians estimate that there may have been as many as fifty regiments of Loyalist troops. They disagree, however, in their estimates of the numbers of men who actually fought with the British against their fellow colonists; perhaps as few as 8,000, perhaps as many as 50,000—the numbers vary widely from source to source. What is accepted as true is that the British found much less active Loyalist support than they had expected to find.

Famous regiments that supported the king include the Loyal American Regiment, formed of New Yorkers; the King's Rangers from New Jersey; and the three-hundred-man First Battalion of Maryland Loyalists. Accounts of the various units speak of the hardships these soldiers encountered, and the fact that desertion to the enemy was common, especially as the war continued. Despised by

Native Americans were often caught in the middle of the conflict, but many of them sided with the British because they were justifiably concerned about colonial expansion. Here, British general John Burgoyne addresses a group of Native Americans.

their fellow colonists, they were often treated with distrust and scorn by their British and Hessian allies for their lack of military skill.

One historian speaks of the general dislike of the Loyalists by the British military, accusing British soldiers of "definite harassment of the Loyalists" and having a "characteristically supercilious" attitude toward them. He does give one officer, Lord Cornwallis, credit for being different: "He treats a Loyalist like his friend, embarked on the same cause."[15] The failure of the British to use these Loyalists wisely, and incorporate their knowledge of

the terrain and types of colonial fighting skills, was yet another factor leading eventually to the British defeat.

All of the soldiers from home shared one trait in common. They were not, at first, professional soldiers, the "regulars" that other countries might field in time of war. These soldiers had only the experience of being militia, citizen soldiers banded together to defend themselves and their local communities. From across the ocean would come the professional soldiers, the regulars, to fight on both sides of this revolutionary conflict.

CHAPTER THREE

The Soldiers From Across the Ocean

An American newspaper in 1775 spread the word that it looked like conflict with the British was now imminent.

Every mark of power is preparing to be shown to the Americans. Three general officers are appointed to go with the next troops. They are Generals Burgoyne, Clinton, and Howe. A considerable number of men are drafted from the three regiments of guards, and ordered to hold themselves in readiness to embark for America immediately. Four regiments from Ireland, one of them light dragoons, are under sailing orders for Boston, with several capital ships of war, and six cutters, to obstruct the American trade, and prevent all European goods from going there, particularly arms and ammunition.[1]

These British troops would be the first of about 50,000 to be sent to the colonies to suppress the rebellion. At any one time over the course of the war, there were rarely more than 20,000 British troops on American soil, but it was always obvious that Britain would be able to muster as many men as needed for the war. These troops, called Redcoats, lobsterbacks, or bloodybacks by the colonists because of their red uniforms, were known to be the best fighting men in the world.

To supplement their forces, the British hired soldiers to fight alongside them in battle. These soldiers, from varying states within the area we now call Germany, were usually referred to as Hessians, since one of the larger groups was hired from the prince of Hesse. About 30,000 of these German soldiers would fight with the British. The Hessians were known as exceptionally well trained and disciplined soldiers and, as such, they were feared by the colonists.

The arriving British soldiers, or at least their officers, seemed to look on the colonists with total contempt. One wrote back, offering his opinion that "the Misled deluded people . . . have been drawn into Ruin, by a set of mock patriots." In a later letter, a friend of his would "curse Columbus and all the discoverers of this Diabolical Country."[2]

Another British officer, responding to a complaint about harassment of civilians in the New York area, was even more bitter in his attack on the Patriots:

As much as I abhor every principle of Inhumanity or ungenerous Conduct, I should, were I in more authority, Burn every Committee Man's House within my reach, as I deem those Agents the wicked instruments of the continued Calamities of this Country. . . . I guess before the end of the next Campaign they will be torn to pieces by their own countrymen whom they have forcibly dragged; in opposition to their Principles and Duty . . . to take up Arms against their Lawfull Sovereign, and compelled them to Exchange their happy constitution, for Paper, Rags, Anarchy and Distress.[3]

It is possible that this contempt for the American rebels and a sure sense of their own superiority is what lost the war for the British. The memoirs of British soldiers repeatedly excuse some Patriot victory as being the result of a surprise attack, a minor fault by a sentry, or supposedly overwhelming numbers of American troops. One soldier writes, after losing one battle, of the Americans having "nearly treble our numbers in the field" and having access to "instant reinforcements,"[4] an assessment that would surely have amused General Washington as he desperately tried to pull together his undersized army.

Even up through the surrender of Cornwallis's army at Yorktown in 1781, the accounts by British soldiers never credit good soldiering by the Americans or effective leadership by their officers. In fact, by the end of the war, the losers were still laying more blame for their defeat on the skill of the Patriots' French allies than on that of the Americans themselves.

One other factor may also have affected the attitudes of the British military: There was not widespread support for this war in Great Britain. Many British agreed with the complaints of the colonists and felt the government should have negotiated a settlement with them. This had made recruitment of soldiers to go to America more difficult. One historian even notes that "some officers refused to serve."[5]

For the Hessian soldiers arriving in America, this was not a war that they had chosen to fight. One historian writes of the reasons for the princes of Germany to sell the services of their troops this way: "With their blood-money the princes were enabled to pay off old debts . . . and they seem to have been quite satisfied. That the soldiers and their families were not so enthusiastic about these bargains did not matter in the least."[6]

There was definitely controversy between the British and their Hessian allies. The British, who seemed to feel superior to everyone else involved, often blamed them for any losses. Hessian General Friedrich von Riedesel, reporting home to his superiors, was quick to comment. "We still lack, however, ammunition, and the most necessary things. . . . It is lamentable that the requisite things for this campaign have not been sent here from England until so

Hessian troops, sold by their duke to fight for the British, march through a German town on their way to board ships to America.

In his writings, General Friedrich von Riedesel was objective about both his British allies and his American opponents.

late. Consequently, a large portion of the time that should have been devoted to the campaign, passes by, and thus this expensive war is prolonged."[7]

Riedesel also was noticing that the British did not seem to understand their enemy and seemed to have too high an opinion of their own abilities. He notes in 1777 that the British have had to replace their general in charge of the campaign to take the Champlain Valley for lack of success and writes of the new commander: "A great deal is said concerning the army of General [William] Howe, especially in regard to its discipline. But I know not how much

we can believe of these reports, for it always seems to me that all is not gold that glitters."[8]

Riedesel gradually came to respect the American troops he was fighting against, but his initial impressions were that they were "a miserable race of men with poor officers. They have no money, only paper: and there is such an excitement and tremble in the provinces themselves, that it is impossible for the confederation to last long." At the same time, however, he recognized that "the colonists have only to prolong the matter as long as possible, in order to cause a great scarcity of provisions and men in the English army."[9]

The American troops may have greatly feared the Hessians early in the war because the Germans' reputation as disciplined and skilled fighters had preceded them. But after defeating them at Saratoga in October 1777, the Americans saw the Germans in a different light. Wrote one Continental soldier after the war:

The Hessians came lumbering in the rear. When were they ever in advance? Indeed their equipments prevented such an anomaly. Their heavy caps were almost equal to the weight of the whole equipment of a light infantry soldier. I looked at these men with commiseration. It was well known that their services had been sold by their own petty princes . . . and handed over to the British government at so much a head, to be transported across the ocean and wage war against a people of whose history and even of whose existence they were ignorant. They were found almost totally unfit for the business they were engaged in. They were unable to march through the woods and encounter the difficulties incident to movements in our then almost unsettled country.[10]

The other group of foreign troops that fought in this war for independence was the French, who were allied with the Americans. The French had a long history of enmity with the British. They had just been defeated by them in the French and Indian War, losing their entire province of Canada (then known as New France) in the process.

From the very beginning the Continental Congress knew that it was very important that they enlist France's support in this fight. The colonies could not maintain their independence without financial and military aid from another of the major powers. They also knew, however, that the king of France would hesitate to support a cause that advocated independence from another royal government, since this might encourage dangerous thinking both at home and in France's own colonies. This fear was a very legitimate one. The French Revolution, which in part followed the ideals of the American Revolution, occurred only a short time after the war ended.

The Continental Congress decided to send ambassadors to encourage French support. Benjamin Franklin was given the task of negotiating a treaty with the French. Franklin's instructions were to "solicit the Court of France for an immediate supply of twenty or thirty thousand muskets and bayonets, and a large supply of ammunition and brass field-pieces, to be sent under convoy by France . . . engage a few good engineers in the service of the United States." It was the hope of the Congress that "France means not to let the United States sink in the present contest"; thus Franklin should counter any arguments "that we are able to support the war on our own strength and resources." Franklin could even hint that if France would not help now, "a reunion with Great Britain may be the consequence of a delay."[11]

Also advocating active French participation was the Marquis de Lafayette, who came to America as an early supporter of George Washington and the American fight for freedom. Already serving with Washington, the marquis returned to France in 1778 to lobby for stronger support and aid to the American cause. General Washington, in reporting Lafayette's departure to the Continental Congress, noted: "I shall always be happy to give such a testimony of his services, as his bravery and conduct on all occasions, entitle him to."[12]

Without the assistance of the French troops, the Patriots might not have had the resources necessary to bring the war to final victory. This does not mean, however, that the allies were always the best of friends or even considered themselves to be equals in the fight. The French offered their aid in order to avenge their defeat by the British, not simply because of support for the American ideals of liberty.

French officers (other than Lafayette) seemed to have a sense of superiority over the American troops similar to that of the British. General Jean Baptiste Donatien de Vimeur, the Count de Rochambeau, gives only grudging praise to Washington and the Continental army in his memoir. His scornful view of the colonists themselves and their sense of their own personal liberty is apparent in his discussion of the difficulties in providing winter quarters for his soldiers "in a free country, where each individual held his own property in such sacred veneration, that General Washington's army . . . were obliged to make shift with the wooden huts which the soldiers built for themselves in the forests." He also spoke of

the good discipline of his own French troops in comparison to the American troops. This he attributed to "the zealous efforts of the generals, the superior officers, and subalterns, but more particularly to the good disposition of the soldiers."

Rochambeau does finally give lukewarm praise for the Americans' military ability at the decisive battle at Yorktown: "I must render the Americans the justice to say, that they conducted themselves with that zeal, courage, and emulation, with which they were never backward, in the important part of the attack entrusted to them, and the more so as they were totally ignorant of the operations of a siege."[13]

It is to George Washington's credit as commander of the Continental army that he was able to work with the aristocratic French leaders and still maintain his own control in the face of their lack of respect for their American allies.

How fragile that control might have been can be seen in the observations of one of the German officers, who noted that Washington kept the armies separate when they were in winter quarters. Jäger Captain Johann Ewald claimed to have heard the French refer to the Americans as "rogues" and expressed his opinion that "many a French grenadier's saber would have been plunged into American blood,"[14] had the soldiers not been kept apart. The captain was, of course, fighting on the

Without the assistance of the French troops, the Patriots might not have had the resources necessary to bring the war to final victory.

other side—the losing side—so perhaps his comments should be taken as an attempt to make the winners look bad. Either way, it is obvious even from the memoirs of the victors that the relationship was often not particularly friendly.

With English, French, and German soldiers fighting, and with financial support from the Dutch and other European powers, this revolution was not just of interest to the Americans. The Continental Congress was successful in making this a European war—one that played old enemies against one another in such a way that it helped Americans achieve what they ultimately fought for—their freedom.

CHAPTER FOUR

Life in a Revolutionary Camp

"I am sick, discontented, and out of humor. Poor food. Hard lodging. Cold weather. Fatigue. Nasty clothes. Nasty cookery. Vomit half my time. . . . There comes a bowl of beef soup, full of burnt leaves and dirt."[1] Continental army doctor Albigence Waldo's diary entry captures perfectly the miseries of camp life during the Revolutionary War.

Of all these miseries, the one that usually drew the most response was the food situation. Only rarely is there a positive comment to be found about food, such as this one from Hessian Johann Ewald, written early in the war: ". . . most excellent provisions of salted beef and pork, peas, butter, rice, and flour for bread . . . the best English beer."[2] Conditions for the Hessians deteriorated as the war continued. The following year, another Hessian would record: "Pork at noon, pork at night, pork cold, pork hot . . . pork was to us a splendid food without which we would have starved to death."[3]

Among the American troops, the situation was at its worst during the winter months. In 1776 on Mount Independence, in what is now Vermont, the troops were without shoes, and the death rate was averaging eight to ten soldiers a day. At Valley Forge in 1778, conditions were terrible:

[A]bout one half of the men were destitute of small clothes, shoes, and stockings; some thousands were without blankets. . . . At one time nearly three thousand men were returned unfit for duty, from the want of clothing, and it was not uncommon to track the march of men over ice and frozen ground, by the blood from their naked feet. Several times during the winter, they experi-

Perhaps the most notorious encampment of the Revolutionary War was that at Valley Forge, Pennsylvania, during the winter of 1776–1777. There, General Washington's troops suffered cold, hunger, and disease as repeated requests for supplies went unmet.

enced little less than a famine in camp. . . . For two or three weeks in succession, the men were on half allowance, and for four or five days without bread, and again as many without beef or pork.[4]

Soldier Ebenezer Huntington wrote to his brother, a fellow officer in the Continental army, about the food situation:

The Provision we draw hath been Chiefly Salt Beef, and that alone without bread or Potatoes is tedious—It appears to me that unless the Army is better Supplied, you had better disband them now. . . . This whole part of the Country are Starving for want of bread. . . . Is it not Possible for the State to do something else besides Promises, Promises cannot feed or Clothe a Man always— Performance is sometimes necessary to make a man believe you intend to Preform.[5]

Huntington's worry about the impact of the shortages on the morale of the soldiers was shared by others. Another Revolutionary War officer, John Laurens, General Washington's aide, had the advantage of knowing that his messages would go directly to the political leaders. Writing to his father, who was president of the Continental Congress at the time, he noted: "We have lately been in a more alarming situation for want of provisions. The soldiers were scarcely restrained from mutiny by the eloquence and management of our officers. Those who are employed to feed us, either for want of knowledge or for want of activity or both, never furnish supplies adequate to our wants. . . . Here of late it has reduced up almost to the point of disbanding."[6]

George Washington, as commander in chief, should have been spending more of his time planning military strategy. Instead, the need for provisions kept him busily writing both to the Continental Congress and to the various states to remind them of the need of the army for proper supplies. The army was lacking not only in basic necessities such as food, clothing, tents, and blankets. At times, Washington could not even obtain enough weapons and ammunition—a definite problem for a military leader trying to fight in the field. One letter to the Continental Congress shows his frustration:

I am exceedingly sorry that I am under the Necessity of applying to you and calling the Attention of Congress to the State of our Arms, which is truly alarming. . . . Unhappy

Situation & much to be deplored especially when we have every Reason to convince us that we have to contend with a formidable Army well provided of every necessary. . . . Our treasury is almost exhausted, and the Demands ag[ains]t it considerable. . . . I wrote to the Gen'l Court yesterday and to the Convention of New Hampshire immediately upon seeing the great Deficiency in our Arms, praying that they would interest themselves in the Matter, and furnish me with all in their Power.[7]

The issue of lack of supplies was a serious one not just because of the need to provision the troops but also for the matter of keeping soldiers in the army. Lack of supplies made the soldiers rebellious and more apt to desert. Rebellious soldiers forced officers to be stricter in administering discipline. Discipline was a major issue for the soldiers and the officers in charge of them. Most military leaders felt that the common soldier needed to be kept constantly under control or he would not be as effective when he got into battle. Soldiers must be trained to obey every order, no matter how small or unreasonable it seemed, so that they would obey the orders given in battle.

Sometimes the complaints about the soldiers' conduct seem strange to us today. An example comes from one of the Orderly Books of the time: "Twas observed Last Evenin, while prayers were attending, that Noise and Singing was made by people who remained in camp, which attended to disturb Public worship. Tis ordered for futer that no noise or Singing Shall be made In Camp nither Shall the Sutlers [suppliers] offer to sell anything during the time of Devine Servise, unless in case of pure necessity."[8]

At another time orders came forbidding card playing in camp "under the penalty of a court-martial . . . for the reason that it is wicked and brings a disgrace on the officers."[9]

At the same time, other orders were given that probably led to the soldiers' becoming unruly in camp, such as this one: "In consequence of the wet weather, the comesary is to isue one gal. of Rum to each non comisind officer and solgier in camp."[10]

Maintaining discipline could be a serious problem. Very little of the soldiers' time was actually spent fighting or even marching. Much of the time was idle and the availability of rum and beer, combined with the card playing and dice games going on, often led to fights. Both armies were concerned about keeping the men in order. The prince of

While it would have been ideal for Washington to focus on battle strategy, during his stay at Valley Forge he had no choice but to deal instead with the crises presented by a lack of supplies for his men. Here, he sees the bloody footprints left in the snow by soldiers with no boots.

Hesse, responding to General Riedesel's latest reports about camp conditions, offers his advice for handling the soldiers: "It will be, as you know, impossible to warrant their zeal in the service, but strict discipline, which I know you make a point to have, will be the best means of making them attend to their duty."[11]

The means of maintaining discipline in both armies was by having military trials, called courts-martial, to handle offenses against the rules of the camp. The records of these trials seem extremely harsh to the reader of today.

At a Gen'l Court Martial . . . Thom^s Lawler of the 4th Penn^l Reg^t also Tried for the Same Crime found Guilty and Sintance to Recieve one Hundred lashes on his beare Back well

Thoms Lawler . . . found Guilty and Sintance to Recieve one Hundred lashes on his beare Back well Laid on. . . .

Laid on. . . . At the same Court Mar^l William Marvis of the 9th Penn^l Reg^t Tried for geting Drunk Threatning the Life of one Cameron and Hutchings and kicking Hutchings Down and also for Stricking the Corporal of the Quat^r Guard when confined. . . . That being a Breach of the 6th articel and 18th Section of the articles of Warr the Court Sintince him to Receive thirty Lahes on his beare Back well Laid on—The Commander in Chief approves of all Those Sintances . . . and orders The Punishment to be Executed to Morrow Morning at Roll Call.[12]

Punishments were just as harsh in the British and Hessian armies. Dr. J. F. Wasmus wrote of seeing two soldiers "knouted," or lashed, and of another forced to "run the gauntlet" eight times, adding, "he died 8 hours later."[13]

Some of the discipline problems in camp also came from worries that the soldiers had about their families left at home. Many cases of desertion had nothing to do with a lack of supplies or losing faith in the American cause. A soldier might simply have received bad news from home and decided he needed to go home for a time to help out. Soldiers could not understand why, if they were not missing any actual fighting, they should not be allowed to go home. Many needed the time off to plant or harvest a crop. They saw the rules as harsh and unreasonable and often decided to leave anyway and accept the punishment when they returned.

One soldier wrote home to his wife: "I am Very uneasy in my mind about you . . . if you Due suffer I am Determined to come Home." Hearing from his wife that his only son was ill, he agonized over whether to leave, finally deciding to stay. "I wish I whas at home with you But insted of Being with you . . . I am obliged to Be hear."[14] It would be a month before he would receive the news that his son had died. He didn't write whether he regretted his decision to stay.

Some soldiers did have their families with them in camp. This was a common military practice in the European armies among the officers. Hessian General Riedesel had his wife and three children with him, and when he was taken prisoner, they went into captivity with him. In the British army, family members were entitled to receive rations along with the soldiers. In 1777, Daniel Weir, the commissary to the British army in America, reported to the government back home the "Numbers Daily Victualed." For his report dated May 17 he noted

23,601 soldiers, 2,776 women, and 1,901 children. Women received half of the men's ration and children received one fourth. Historians estimate that about 5,000 military wives traveled with the British army during the course of the war.[15] The military commanders made use of these women as cooks, laundresses, and seamstresses and to help in the care of the sick. Some even received payment for their services.

There were fewer woman and children traveling with the American army, although in cases where their homes had been destroyed or they were in territory occupied by the British, families did sometimes stay with their soldiers. In 1777, Washington issued an order to his officers "to use every reasonable method in their power to get rid" of family members because they were "a clog upon every movement," and "every incumbrance proves greatly prejudicial to the service."[16] Later orders forbade the women to ride in the baggage wagons or march with the soldiers.

The rules could be more lenient when the soldiers were in winter quarters. At the time of the Revolutionary War, armies tended not to fight in the winter because of transportation problems. The generals would select a site for the soldiers to camp for the winter. In some cases, soldiers were actually sent home. This was true at Mount Independence in the

The military commanders made use of these women as cooks, laundresses, and seamstresses, and to help in the care of the sick.

winter of 1776–1777, when the number of soldiers dropped from ten thousand to about three thousand. If the soldiers were home, they would not be using up scarce supplies.

For winter quarters, the soldiers usually built themselves log huts. Continental army surgeon Dr.

James Thacher speaks of the winter of 1778–1779 and the delay in getting into winter quarters. "Having continued to live under cover of canvass tents most of the winter, we have suffered extremely from exposure to cold and storms." The log houses that he describes the soldiers building are typically "constructed with the trunks of trees, cut into various lengths . . . the roof is formed of similar pieces of timber . . . the vacancies between the logs are filled in with plastering consisting of mud and clay." He notes that the huts for officers hold only three or four men, while those for soldiers "have but one room, and contain ten or twelve men."[17] After the building itself was complete, "wooden bunks were made. These were elevated off the dirt floor to protect against the cold and dampness."[18] Covered with straw, the bunks would seem the height of luxury after sleeping on the ground during the fighting season.

The life of a soldier in either army was hard. But the officers knew that they needed their soldiers fit to fight and also willing to fight. Thus they ran the camps with discipline, but also with determination to fight with their superiors to get the soldiers the things they needed to keep them content enough to remain in the army.

CHAPTER FIVE

Disease and Death in Camp

"Visited the sick in camp, found near one half the Reg^t unfit for duty, and many whose situation was truly dangerous. The dysentery, Jaundice, Putrid, intermitting, & Billious fevers, were the principal diseases that attended the troops, which proved fatal in a variety of instances," recorded Dr. Lewis Beebe in his diary on September 1, 1776.[1] His was not an uncommon complaint from doctors remembering the conditions of the soldiers during the Revolutionary War.

Disease was the most common cause of death among the soldiers during the war. Perhaps as many as seven out of every eight deaths were from disease. Dr. Beebe recorded the most common causes of death once the soldiers were in camp and used to soldiering. Among the new soldiers just arriving, there were also truly horrible outbreaks of smallpox. Vaccination of the general public to prevent small-

pox was the great medical achievement of the time. However, the great majority of people had not been vaccinated. This was because the process of vaccinating, done by inoculating the person with actual smallpox, causing them to suffer a mild form of the disease, was dangerous in itself. It was also a more common event in larger cities. With most soldiers arriving from small towns around the colonies where vaccinations were not readily available, smallpox raged through the camps. It was very contagious, and many died from the disease.

Doctors traveling with the British and Hessian armies had additional problems to treat in their soldiers. Soldiers from Europe were not used to the extremes of temperature in the colonies and often became quite ill after arrival. Dr. Johann David Schoepff commented: "Most new-comers to this country have to pay tribute to the climate by some indisposition or other, especially if they land during the hot season of the year. Our troops arrived here in July. From that time till October most of our men were, one after another, in the hospitals of New York, or in the regimental hospitals on Staaten-Eyland or at Harlem; there were very few who escaped without an attack of dysentery fever."[2]

It is sometimes hard to imagine what medical conditions were like at the time. First it is important to understand that even medical schools were a new addition to the colonies. Most doctors trained by serving as apprentices to older doctors. Education was limited to whatever conditions were suffered by the patients his mentor happened to see in the three or four years the prospective doctor spent as an apprentice. This was a time when dissection of cadavers (dead bodies) was very rare, so most doctors were just guessing as to what might be happening inside the human body. There was no anesthesia available, and thus surgical procedures were done only in dire emergencies. Doctors still knew little about how diseases were transmitted, although many were trying to find conditions that hampered the spread of diseases. The most common treatments were bloodletting and the use of various herbs.

Bleeding the patient was actually the treatment of choice for just about *any* illness or injury. One Scottish doctor, William Buchan, whose work would have been read by American doctors of the time, is quoted as recommending this approach for "inflammatory fevers . . . all typical inflammations . . . asthmas, sciatic pains, coughs, head-aches, rheumatism, the apoplexy, and bloody flux . . . fits, blows, bruises, or any violent hurt received."[3] Doctors used a lancet to open a vein and drain several ounces of blood from the patient. If the patient did not get better, the procedure would be done again repeatedly.

In addition to the bleeding, medicines were used. Most of them had been used for centuries, and many probably harmed more patients than they ever helped. Opium and laudanum were used to relieve pain; and quinine was employed to treat malaria. These medicines, when given in the correct dosages, could be effective. Alcohol, in the form of beer, rum, and wine, was often used as a medicine, even though it probably was not of any real help to the patient. The doctors often used purgatives, which were substances that they believed could drive the disease from the body. These might make a person vomit or bring on a violent case of diarrhea. Most often the results only weakened the patient and made him sicker.

Even so, the doctors of the day were not fools. They attempted constantly to add to their knowledge and come up with some way to ease the conditions of the soldiers they saw as patients. Dr. Schoepff shared his frustration about one such situation for which he had no treatment available: "The battle near Monmouth, on June 28, 1778, was remarkable from one circumstance which has not its parallel in the history of the New World; without receiving a wound, fifty-nine men fell on our side solely from the extraordinary heat and fatigue of the day; and many on the side of the rebels succumbed to the same causes, in spite of the men being more accustomed to the climate."[4]

Another doctor, James Thacher, thought it important to note that "these brave men, while in the service of their country, receive in sickness all the kind attention from physicians and nurses, which their circumstances require, they have the prayers and consolations of pious clergymen, and are destitute of nothing."[5]

One of the serious problems caused by the rate of disease was the impact it had on the morale of the other soldiers. Watching those around them suffer and knowing that they, too, would probably fall victim to several severe episodes of disease during their time as soldiers made it harder for them to remain. They often recorded their horror at what they were seeing—horror probably made worse by knowing it could be them lying there helpless. Soldier Bayze

Wells recorded one such scene in his journal: "About 1,500 Sick men were ordered to this Place oh the Groans of the Sick. What they undergo I Cant Express. Nither is it in the Power of Man to Give any Idea of the Distresses of them Laying on the Ground nothing to Cover them but the Heavens and Wet Cool weather."[6]

Noted one doctor of the medical conditions while on the march:

> Many of us were now in a sad plight with the diarrhoea. Our water was of the worst quality. The lake was low, surrounded with mountains, situate in a low morass. Water was quite yellow. With this we were obliged not only to do all our cooking, but use it as our constant drink. Nor would a little of it suffice, as we were obliged to eat our meat exceedingly salt. This with our constant fatigue called for large quantities of drink. No sooner had it got down than it was puked up by many of the poor fellows.[7]

The doctors may have been doing their best with the skills and knowledge of the time. However, the disease rate for both sides shows that the soldiers paid a terrible cost in illness and death for their military service.

Without receiving a wound, fifty-nine men fell on our side solely from the extraordinary heat and fatigue of the day.

CHAPTER SIX

On the March

"Shall inform you that I injoye my health, but am so Fatigued by an insessant marching that should it continue I fear I shall be relaxed and reduced to that degre I shall not be able to do duty in the Field," wrote Massachusetts Lieutenant Benjamin Gilbert in a letter home on July 3, 1781.[1] Marching during the Revolutionary War was a terrible burden on the soldiers in a country that was only sparsely settled and still depended on rivers for most transportation.

At the beginning of the war, roads in the colonies were the best they had ever been. However, it is important to remember that when settlement began in the early 1600s, the only roads that existed were hunting trails used by the native peoples. By the time of the Revolution, actual roads connected the colonies. People were able to travel from Massachusetts to Georgia riding in stagecoaches.

The journey might last a month, but at least one could get from place to place traveling by "stages," staying overnight at inns along the way.

That system, of course, did not work well if one was trying to move an army. The best system for moving an army was by water. That meant that the war, especially in its early stages, would depend on control of the rivers and other natural transportation corridors. This system favored the British with their strong navy. When the British were forced to evacuate Boston in 1776, they simply loaded the soldiers onto ships and moved the army to Canada. Later, when they occupied New York City, they arrived by water.

In spite of using waterways where possible, much of the time the armies found themselves forced to travel by land through densely forested areas. The reminiscences of the soldiers reflect the

Moving troops by water was far easier than having them march on crude roads and through dense forest. It was especially easy for the British, who had a superior navy and plenty of vessels. Here, British troops land at New Jersey on the Hudson River in late 1776.

frustration they felt at the prolonged marching and its side effects.

Wrote Redcoat John Enys: "What a disagreable March . . . our way laying through Swamps and broken grownd with an emmence Number of fallen Trees, over which [we] were continualy falling as it was so very dark. . . . This kind of Marching is as uncertain as it is Slow and disagreeable."[2]

Yankee Doodle Private Joseph Plumb Martin would agree wholeheartedly with his enemy's description and top it with his own tale of the end of a day's march: "It was then foggy and the water dropping from the trees like a shower. We endeavored to get fire . . . failing, we were forced by our old master, Necessity, to lay down and sleep if we could, with three others of our constant companions, Fatigue, Hunger, and Cold."[3]

The soldiers complained of the weather on the march, the fact that supplies never kept up with them, and that often they were forced to retrace their march since either the directions were wrong or the orders had changed. They responded to the situation with humor on occasion, as did Doctor Isaac Senter in his comment on a long march: "By this time our feet began to be very sensible of our undertaking."[4] Senter maintains his sense of humor as he describes the end of their march, when they actually got to board ships.

With his fellow soldiers he found that sailing had its own hazards: "That evening heavy wind with considerable rain, this bringing on a swell, occasioned most of the troops to disgorge themselves of their luxuries so plentifully laid in ere we embarked."[5]

The enemy could also find amusement of sorts in the marching conditions. One Hessian prisoner reported marching to a village where there was not enough housing to bring the troops indoors. He concludes of their night outside: "We got so covered with frost . . . that we looked like great sugar dolls."[6]

On a more serious note, one Redcoat, Thomas Hughes, puts part of the blame for the British loss at Saratoga on the road conditions that made marching large armies impossible. He notes twice in a few days in his journal their need to stop while "proper roads were cut for the troops, to march through the wood, which was thick, and in several places swamps."[7]

General Riedesel reported home to the prince of Hesse on some of the difficulties caused by the terrain: "Aside from a few cultivated regions on the rivers, all the hills are covered with woods. All we can do, therefore, is to post ourselves near rivers, take forts, and build new ones, and go with the Indians as much as possible through the primeval forests in order to destroy communications."[8] For these professional soldiers, the terrain, which favored

*One Redcoat
puts part of the blame for the
British loss at Saratoga on the road conditions
that made marching large armies impossible.*

the colonial army, was one more reason for finding the fight difficult. For armies trained in open-field battle, this long slogging through marsh and woods helped to defeat them before they ever got a chance to meet the enemy and attack him decisively.

Those same factors that made marching such a miserable experience for both sides would give the advantage to the colonial militias and the Continental army over the long term. The impassable roads would help them win the war.

CHAPTER SEVEN

Words From the Field

"This was the first time in my life that I had witnessed the awful scene of a battle, when man was engaged to destroy his fellow-man. I well remembered my sensations on the occasion, for they were solemn beyond description, and very hardly could I bring my mind to be willing to attempt the life of a fellow-creature."[1] Colonel Benjamin Tallmadge, who would become Washington's chief of intelligence, had thoughts on his first battle experience that were probably similar to those of many in the Continental army. Unlike the trained Redcoats and Hessians, war was not the primary occupation of the Patriot troops. These farm boys turned soldiers must have found the transition extremely difficult when they first went into battle.

The fact that many soldiers had difficulty actually fighting was enough of a problem that George Washington found it necessary to issue a special order in September 1777: "If, in any time of action, any man who is not wounded, whether he has arms or not, turns his back on the enemy, and attempts to run away or retreat before orders are given for it, those officers are instantly to put him to death. The man does not deserve to live who basely flies, breaks his solemn engagement, and betrays his country."[2]

The words of the soldiers written after the battles convey their heroism along with their fears. They show that most fought their war with a steady determination. There would be talk along the way of desertion or leaving the cause, and some soldiers actually did so, the most notable being General Benedict Arnold, a true hero of the early part of the war who ultimately ended up serving in the British army. However, for the most part, the soldiers on both sides of the conflict did their duty.

That duty began on April 19, 1775, when the British troops moved out of Boston seeking to arrest the Massachusetts leaders of the rebellion and destroy their military supplies. The militia—the minutemen—met the British army at Lexington. At eleven that morning word of the attack was sent to all the surrounding towns: "To all friends of American Liberty, be it known, that this morning before break of day, a Brigade, consisting of about 1,000 or 1,200 men, landed at Phipp's Farm at Cambridge, and marched to Lexington, where they found a Company of our Militia in Arms, upon whom they fired without any provocation and killed 6 Men and Wounded 4 others."[3]

Samuel Haws was a member of the Wrentham, Massachusetts, militia who received the "alarm" on that day. He remembers: "About one a clock the minute men were alarmed and met at Landlord Moons. We marched from there . . . towards Roxbury for we heard that the regulars had gone out and had killed six men and had wounded Some more that was at Lexington then the kings troops proceded to concord and there they were Defeated and Drove Back fiting as they went they gat to charlstown hill that night."[4]

Militiamen stand at the ready as British troops advance at Lexington. After this first battle of the war, the need for a regular army was evident. The Americans needed a large, organized, and mobile force to replace the local militias that had traditionally protected their own home areas.

With war finally arriving, there was an immediate need for an army of regulars to take the place of the militias, which were only intended to protect their own communities. These regulars, as formal soldier swere called to distinguish them from the militia, would eventually become the Continental army. Minuteman Haws reports the "inlistment" arriving on April 27, only eight days after the first battle. He also records a series of alarms over the next several days, showing that this attack was not unique and that the British regulars, the hated Redcoats, or lobsterbacks, intended to destroy the rebellion.

The next encounter, and the first major battle of the Revolutionary War, occurred on June 17. The Americans had fortified a position for themselves on Breed's Hill (although the battle would mistakenly be known as the Battle of Bunker Hill) overlooking Boston. The British attacked in order to remove this threat. To the Redcoats' great surprise, the Patriots actually were able to resist the attack and drive back the British with heavy casualties on their first two attempts to take the hill. But the Americans did not have the ammunition to maintain their position, and the third attack of the British was successful.

Abigail Adams collected accounts of the battle, so that her husband, John, a delegate to the Continental Congress and future president of the United States, could have accurate information to pass on to the other delegates. After sending him a quick note that she acknowledged was more rumor than fact, she sent the following account on June 25:

> When we consider all the circumstances, attending this action, we stand astonished that our people were not all cut off. They had but one hundred feet entrenched, the number who were engaged did not exceed eight hundred, and they with not half ammunition enough; the reinforcement not able to get to them seasonably. The tide was up, and high, so that their floating batteries came upon each side of the causeway, and their row-galleys kept a continual fire. Added to this, the fire from Cops Hill, and from the ships; the town in flames, all around them, and the heat from the flames so intense as scarcely to be borne; the day one of the hottest we have had this season, and the wind blowing the smoke in their faces,— only figure to yourself all these circumstances, and then consider that we do not count sixty men lost.[5]

She estimated the British dead at 1,400 or so. Even though she was trying to be accurate, later counts said the British lost more than 1,000 soldiers

To the Redcoats' great surprise, the Patriots actually were able to resist the attack and drive back the British with heavy casualties on their first two attempts to take the hill.

and the Americans had about 400 killed or wounded. News of the battle unified the resistance in the colonies against Great Britain. The Continental Congress had appointed George Washington as commander of an army that he would have to establish only three days before the battle, and now Washington traveled to Boston to take command.

In May 1775, Ethan Allen and his Green Mountain Boys had decided that if war had indeed broken out, the American forces would need to control the Champlain Valley in what is now western Vermont and eastern upstate New York. On his own initiative, Allen headed to Fort Ticonderoga, and, joined by Benedict Arnold, captured the fort from the British. Two things would result from this successful assault. The most important was that the cannons from the fort would be transported overland to Boston and would be used to force the British from their stronghold there the next spring. The second impact was that Arnold's success led him to feel he could possibly capture Montreal in Canada. Since Montreal would be the main staging area for an attack by the British into the New England area, this was a good idea. The problem was that it was not well planned or executed.

Isaac Senter was a soldier in this campaign. The campaign did not allow for the territory that the sol-diers would be forced to cross, thus delaying their arrival. Disease was rampant among the soldiers, weakening the army greatly. There was a lack of coordination between the two groups who would make the attack. Everything that could go wrong actually did. Colonel (later General) Benedict Arnold's part of the attack on December 31, 1775, was initially successful, but General Richard Montgomery, who was in charge of the other attack, was killed, and his soldiers never arrived. Unable to hold their position without support from Montgomery's troops, and with their weapons wet and thus misfiring (if they would fire at all), the Americans were forced to surrender.

Several days later, the remaining parts of the army were forced to retreat. Senter recorded the scene in his journal:

The army was in such a scattered condition as rendered it impossible to collect them either for a regular retreat, or to bring them into action. In this dilemma, orders were given to as many of the troops to retreat as the time would permit, and in the most irregular, *helter skelter* manner we raised the siege, leaving every thing. All the camp equipage, ammunition, and even our cloth-

The idea behind the Montreal campaign was sound, but it turned into a disaster for the Continental army. This illustration shows an attack led by Colonel Benedict Arnold, who later found success at the Battle of Saratoga before disgracing himself by turning traitor and fighting actively for the British.

ing, except what little we happened to have on us. . . . They still kept in chase of us. . . . The most of our sick fell into their hands. . . . No conveniences for ferrying our troops over the rivers emptying in upon either side of the St. Lawrence, except a canoe or two. . . . Thus ended an expedition of nine months continuance, the ill success of which in any other cause would have induced us to have renounced the principles.[6]

It was not a good end for the first fighting season for the American forces in the northern colonies.

There had been more success in the southern colonies. An attempt by the colonial governor of Virginia, Lord Dunmore, to suppress the rebellion in his state ended in failure. Loyalists in North Carolina would suffer their own defeat in February 1776 at Moore's Creek Bridge. There would be an attempt to take Charleston, South Carolina, in June 1776, but that also would fail, and the British troops would return to the North.

The loyalty of many of these southern colonists to the American cause was stronger and more determined than the British had assumed. In one instance, a South Carolina militiaman named Josiah Culbertson, assigned to guard an ammunition stor-age area, found himself alone with only his mother-in-law to assist in protecting the house from an attack by about 150 British troops: "Great as the hazard was, rather than give it up . . . loaded his guns and, while his mother-in-law was employed in running him a supply of bullets, kept up such a fire upon the Tories from the house that they . . . retreated, leaving himself, his mother-in-law, and the ammunition safe."[7]

Facing this kind of fanatical opposition, the British decided that they would be more successful if they divided the colonies and destroyed the opposition in the North first. For the next two years, most of the action would take place in the northern part of the colonies. It would begin with a major British defeat.

The cannons from Fort Ticonderoga were installed on Dorchester Heights overlooking Boston, with the work completed on the night of March 4, 1776. Yankee Doodle Lieutenant Isaac Bangs was there and remembered when the firing of the British became a personal attack for him: "At Length a Shot which fell near the Fort by its fall took a different direction and came immediately where I was standing; it hopped after its first Falling about 4 times, & if it had hop[p]ed again before it broke, as its Velocity was diminishing, it would have come, as

A South Carolina militiaman named Josiah Culbertson, assigned to guard an ammunition storage area, found himself alone with only his mother-in-law to assist in protecting the house from an attack.

near as I can judge, to the very Spot where I was; it broke about 25 Yard Distance, and one of the Pieces came with great rapidity about 2 Yards above my Head."[8]

With cannons in place above the city, British General William Howe had no choice but to remove his troops from Boston, and this he did, having them transported by ship to Canada. One Redcoat called it "awfull and Malencholy" and expressed his view that Boston should not have been spared by the evacuating army "as it was there the seeds of Sedition was first Sown, Nursed and Cherish'd."[9]

The British now attempted a strategy to divide the hated New England colonies from the rest of the country. Doing so, they felt, would end the rebellion. Their plan involved a two-part attack. British troops would come south up Lake Champlain and then the Hudson River, while other troops would move north and west from New York City to meet them. General Washington and his Continental army would be responsible for keeping the New York City contingent from reaching Albany. General Benedict Arnold had his own plan for stopping the British arriving from Canada.

Arnold knew that the British would travel from Canada along Lake Champlain. He proposed fortifying the lake at its narrowest point and building a fleet to take on the British navy and delay their progress south. It was a truly bold plan and should not have met with the success it did. The Americans chose a hill opposite Fort Ticonderoga and began to construct a fort there. When word came of the Declaration of Independence in July 1776, it was decided to name the fort Mount Independence.

At the same time, a small fleet of gunboats was being built, and crews were picked to fight in them. The gunboats would sail north to try to harass the British fleet, which was far larger, more powerful, and generally much too big to actually be stopped.

As expected, when the two fleets met, Arnold and his small group of seventeen boats could not defeat the British. They did, however, delay them and actually held their own relatively well given that they were outnumbered and outgunned. When the British then stopped to occupy the old fort at Crown Point, they were further delayed.

By the time the British finally approached Fort Ticonderoga and Mount Independence, it was late fall, and British General Guy Carleton was "saluted with five cannon," in the words of one Yankee Doodle. The general decided that the war would have to wait until spring and retreated back into Canada. Continued Captain Persifer Frazer in his letter home to his wife: "Thus have we disappointed their two grand armies from forming a junction which appears to have been their chief design & would have been attended with unhappy consequences."[10]

The British saw the fighting season as a victory. Redcoat Thomas Hughes wrote of their decision to winter in Canada: "The lake being in our possession."[11] This was, of course, true. The problem was that their best chance to win the entire war had passed. When they returned in the spring, they would meet with some success, but it would lead to a major defeat.

The success of Arnold's strategy was critical because General Washington's attempt to contain the other part of the British army had met with little success. Washington had moved his army to New York City after the British evacuated Boston, guessing correctly that the next attack would come there. He expected to be outnumbered and to have to retreat. Indeed that is what happened.

Yankee Doodle Benjamin Tallmadge recalled the scene as their 10,000-man army faced a force of 25,000 combined Redcoats and Hessian troops: "Before such an overwhelming force of disciplined troops, our small band could not maintain their ground, and the main body retired within their lines at Brooklyn." As the troops retreated, Tallmadge bitterly records: "I also lost a brother the same day, who

The Americans retreat from Long Island, New York, after being overwhelmed and outnumbered more than two to one by British and Hessian troops in a confrontation during Washington's campaign to halt the British from advancing north.

fell into their hands, and was afterwards literally starved to death in one of their prisons; nor would the enemy suffer relief from his friends to be afforded him."[12] The Continental army was gradually pushed back from New York City with the Redcoats under General Howe following.

The battle continued through the fall and early winter with Washington's Continental army gradually being worn away. He lost a large group of his men—about three thousand were captured at the Battle of Fort Washington in November—men who could have helped to keep the British forces divided. Yankee Doodle Quartermaster William Jennison of Massachusetts records some of the retreat in his diary entry for October 28:

> At early dawn we began to move towards the White plains, falling Trees into the Road and casting Stones and whatever might obstruct the Ordnance of the Enemy—the Party arrives at 9 am—At 11 am the Enemy's Light Horse said to have been 800 strong hove in sight on a Ridge of Hills South of the River Bronx (but fordable) which lay between the American Camp and the Ridge—They maneuvered a little while when Gen'l Knox complimented them with a Six [cannonball].

> . . . Had the Enemy continued to keep the main Road for One mile, they must have taken all the Provisions collected for the American Army, but by filing off to the left, a chance was left for us to get most of them to a safer place.[13]

By December the British forces had forced the weakened Continental army through New Jersey with their backs against the Delaware River separating them from Pennsylvania. Delaware Captain Enoch Anderson was part of what he called "the crisis of American danger," and he wrote of the experience after the war: "The British were now in chase of us with twenty thousand men, within three miles of us. We continued on our retreat . . . tearing up bridges and cutting down trees, to impede the march of the enemy. . . . In the afternoon of the next day, we crossed the Delaware into Pennsylvania, and in two hours afterwards the British appeared on the opposite band and cannonaded us. . . . This night we lay amongst the leaves without tents or blankets. . . . It was very cold."[14]

The British, feeling that certain victory was theirs, and that they could finish off the American army in the spring, began settling down for the winter. However, General Washington may have retreated, but his army was not defeated. In a daring move, on the morning of December 26, he recrossed the river and surprised the Hessians holding Trenton, killing a number of them and taking the remainder prisoner. It was a brilliantly conceived attack that gave his army a needed boost to their morale. He followed up his victory with another sneak attack, this time defeating the Redcoats at Princeton.

The year 1776 had been a rough one for the Patriot cause, but the combination of Arnold's and Washington's delaying tactics had prevented the British from joining forces and destroying the colonial rebellion. The next year, 1777, would prove to be critical in determining the outcome of the war.

Yankee Doodle Anderson did not spend this winter with the army. He was assigned to recruiting. After news spread of Washington's successes at Trenton and Princeton, "it went on more briskly . . . and my company was complete early in the spring . . . new regimentals, new arms and fully supplied with ammunition,—and now fitted for war and to try a new campaign."[15]

Other officers were doing the same thing: recruiting, training, and equipping their soldiers for the coming attacks. "The British," wrote Dr. James Thacher, "considered the Continental army as on the point of annihilation, and flattered themselves that what they term the rebellion, is effectually crushed."[16] The British would be shocked when the spring found not a defeated rebellion but a renewed determination to fight this war through.

The Continental army would not always be victorious, but the year would hold more good than bad for them. Washington and his troops continued to harass the British. The British successfully defeated the Continental army in September and took Philadelphia, the capital of the new nation. But they would not hold it for long.

Up north, a new British general, John Burgoyne, was leading the combined British and Hessian attack to divide the colonies. He confidently sailed south into Lake Champlain, took Fort Ticonderoga and Mount Independence without a fight, fought the retreating Americans and defeated them at Hubbardton, and then proceeded to make the same mistake that Carleton had made the previous year. He took his time, settling in and rebuilding his forces, waiting for reinforcements that would greatly increase the size of his army. But this gave the Patriots time to acquire reinforcements also. When the two armies finally met at Saratoga in the fall, it was General Burgoyne who sent the message requesting surrender terms to General Horatio Gates, in charge of the American forces: "impelled by humanity, and . . . justified by established principles and precedents of state and of war, to spare the lives of brave men on honorable terms."[17]

This was a battle that the Americans could never have dreamed of winning, and one that the British should never have lost. The losers blamed it on several factors, including the weather. Wrote one Hessian: "From this time on we moved out every morning an hour before dawn and enjoyed the fresh morning air consisting of heavy hoar frost and then mist which you could actually grasp with your hands. . . . By day there was heat enough to melt you." He further complains of lack of supplies: "There is nothing in this desert, and the enemy would not let anything come from Albany." Finally, he lays the blame on a series of "misfortunes."[18]

The American accounts may give us a clue as to why the Patriots succeeded. Thacher speaks of General Gates being "determined to march and confront his formidable enemy, and endeavor to force him and his troops back to Canada." He writes bravely in his diary: "A terrible conflict is daily expected, both parties appear to be determined to commence the work of destruction." The next day, he records "a very sanguinary battle . . . our troops behaved with that undaunted bravery which has secured to them the victory. . . . Few battles have been more obstinate and unyielding."[19]

General Gates, commonly known as Granny Gates for his timidness in the face of battle, had General Benedict Arnold urging him on at Saratoga. In fact, it was General Arnold who, defying Gates's order, impetuously led a charge on the key British position that brought the American army victory. Perhaps the real story of this most crucial victory is simply that it would be won by whichever side had the nerve to fight it boldly and with confidence. That bold victor was the American side. General Burgoyne had no choice but surrender.

Baroness Riedesel, traveling with her husband, commander of the Hessian troops, wrote of the surrender ceremony: "On the 17th of October, the capitulation was carried into effect. The generals waited upon the American general Gates, and the troops surrendered themselves prisoner of war and laid down their arms . . . while riding through the American camp, was gratified to observe that no body looked at us with disrespect, but, on the contrary, greeted us, and seemed touched at the sight of a captive mother with three children."[20] The Hessian soldiers and their family members would remain prisoners until the end of the war.

This smashing victory at Saratoga would bring the French into the conflict in support of the American cause. But as 1777 came to an end, in some ways it appeared that the Americans were los-

The victory at Saratoga resulted in France joining the war on the side of the Americans, and in other nations sending aid and lending support to the cause. From the Prussian military came Baron Friedrich von Steuben, who trained Washington's troops at Valley Forge in the spring of 1778.

ing. Two of their major cities, New York and their capital, Philadelphia, were now occupied by the British. The American army was enduring a terrible winter, lacking in supplies and demoralized, at Valley Forge, Pennsylvania. However, the decision of the French to enter the conflict would change all of that. Other friendly nations would now also be sending money and supplies. A Prussian military officer, the Baron Friedrich von Steuben, would arrive at Valley Forge and spend the spring training the Continental army in how to fight effectively against the British on open battlefields. French Marquis de Lafayette also arrived and enthusiastically offered his services.

With the French actively involved in the war, Great Britain was forced to guard her other colonies. With fewer resources available, the new British commander, General Henry Clinton, decided to abandon Philadelphia and consolidate his hold on New Jersey and New York. Washington's army harassed his retreat, and the two armies met in a grueling battle on June 28, 1778, at Monmouth Court House, New Jersey. Yankee Doodle Jeremiah Greenman was there on that dreadfully hot day: "[T]hay form'd in a Sollid Collum then fir'd a volley att us . . . we began a fire on them very heavy. . . . Left the Ground with about a thousand kil'd & wounded. on our Side about two hundred kil'd & wounded & died with heat."[21] Another Yankee Doodle, Henry Dearborn, explains the decision not to follow the retreating British: "Our men being beat out with heat & fateague it was thought not Prudent to Persue them."[22]

Although no one truly won this battle, the British definitely lost. When the British finally arrived back in New York City, they had left for the last time until they surrendered the city after the war ended.

Now the British would find themselves the defenders rather than the attackers. One of their major forts, at Stony Point, New York, fell to a surprise American attack in July 1779 by General Anthony Wayne "taking by assault the enemy's fortified post . . . and with the point of the bayonet alone, forcing the garrison to surrender at discretion, not one man escaping."[23] The Americans then were able to force the British to evacuate another fortified position in Newport, Rhode Island, in October 1779. The one city they could not seem to take was New York, but the American forces had at least contained the British.

While Washington and the Continental army were effectively ending the Revolutionary War in the northern and middle colonies, the British were beginning to concentrate their efforts in the southern colonies. Late in 1778 the British took Savannah, Georgia. American troops were not able to take it back in battles in 1779. In 1780 the British moved north into South Carolina, and the American army in the South was forced to surrender at Charleston. This was a terrible loss for the American cause.

Further disaster followed. The Continental Congress appointed General Horatio Gates to command the southern soldiers of the American army. In August 1780, Gates was "totally defeated, in a general action with Lord Cornwallis," wrote Dr. James Thacher. He "retreated with precipitation to the distance of eighty miles, to escape the pursuit of the enemy. This mortifying disaster gives a severe shock to our army."[24]

The southerners redeemed themselves quickly in a brutal battle at Kings Mountain two months later. Killing more than 150 British and taking 700 prisoners and substantial supplies, the Americans had only 28 deaths and 64 wounded. One of those American deaths was that of Preston Goforth of North Carolina. On the same day, three of his brothers also died in the same battle, fighting as Loyalists. British General Clinton heard the news of the defeat at Kings Mountain at his headquarters in New York. He would later write that this was "the first link of a chain of evils that followed each other in regular succession until they at last ended in the total loss of America."[25]

Three months later, in January 1781, the next link in the chain was forged. Dr. Thacher recorded in his diary on January 10: "Accounts have been received, that an action has been fought at a place called the Cowpens, in Carolina . . . the enemy were totally routed and pursued upwards of twenty miles. . . . Morgan and his party have acquired immortal honor."[26]

The next meeting of the two armies in the South would be a victory for neither. The battle at Guilford Courthouse, North Carolina, on March 15, 1781, was Cornwallis's attempt to avenge his recent losses. The British did hold the field at the end of the battle, but it was not a victory. The American strategy in the South now was to avoid open battle. Instead, the American forces under General Nathanael Greene constantly harassed the British soldiers. Whenever possible, Cornwallis would force an encounter and the British would win, but never decisively. The Americans were winning a war of attrition as they began to wear down the British forces.

General Cornwallis's commander, General Clinton, watching this action from the safety of New York City, was also frustrated. He feared that all of this chasing after the American forces was simply a diversion to force him to send more men to assist Cornwallis, and then be attacked himself. He unwisely ordered Cornwallis into Virginia to a port where men could be loaded into boats for transport. In doing so, he accidentally set the stage for the final major conflict of the war—the meeting of the British with the combined American and French forces at Yorktown in the fall of 1781. The last link was falling into place.

During all of this, there were also battles being fought in the western parts of the colonies—areas that are now Ohio, Illinois, and Indiana. These were not on the scale of the major battles in the East, but they drew off resources that might have been used to end the war

A regiment from Maryland retakes a cannon lost in the Battle of Guilford Courthouse, North Carolina, in 1781.

more quickly. There were also naval engagements taking place and American victories against the world's greatest navy. Captain John Paul Jones, the father of the American navy, constantly harassed British shipping and even managed to capture a large British warship, the *Serapis*, in a battle off the Yorkshire coast of Great Britain, which sank his own ship.

Throughout the war, soldiers fought on different fronts, most often in small, largely unremembered battles. However, taken as a whole, these battles combined to raise the cost and effort for the British in their attempt to keep the colonies to the point that they ultimately decided that it was not worth continuing the fight.

CHAPTER EIGHT

Wounded or Killed

"I stepped and was in the act of cocking my gun when his bayonet . . . gave me a thrust through my hand and into my thigh . . . pulled the bayonet out of my thigh, but it hung to my hand. . . . The thrust gave me much pain, but the pulling of it was much more severe."[1] Yankee Doodle soldier Robert Henry suffered his injury from a British soldier while fighting in South Carolina. One can only imagine the pain as he describes escaping from the field after his injury.

Treatment for wounds, whether from a bayonet, like Henry's, or from a musket ball, was primitive at the time of the American Revolution. Dr. John Jones of New York published a textbook for doctors in 1776, *Plain Concise Practical Remarks on the Treatment of Wounds and Fractures,* which would have been the main source of information for those American physicians who cared for wounded soldiers. In his book, which he specifies is "designed for the use of young Military and Naval Surgeons in North-America," Jones strongly advises his reader to "peruse the sixth commandment, which is 'Thou shalt not kill.' "[2] The advice seems out of place in a medical textbook, but it was actually very appropriate at the time.

Most of those who would be caring for the wounded did not have the experience they would need to know about the damage done by a musket ball, sword, or bayonet to the tissues of the body. Furthermore, they would not know how to help the body heal more quickly from such an injury. Dr. Jones gives very practical advice and reminds these doctors that "many wounds also in themselves not mortal, may be rendered so by neglect or erroneous treatment . . . when the multiplicity of cases prevents the Surgeons from paying a proper attention."[3]

Dr. Jones gives the surgeons detailed instructions on how to examine a wound, how to care for it, and what to expect to happen as the body reacts to the injury. All of this reads very well and seems very modern in terms of techniques—Dr. Jones even notes that patients do better when a doctor is careful with cleanliness. This puts him on the track of the concept of disease-causing germs that would not be proven for another hundred years. But there is a passage that reminds the modern reader of how little even the most competent doctors knew at the time of the Revolutionary War. Dr. Jones writes: "About the fourth day, sooner or later, according to the age of the patient and heat of the weather, a white, pinguious, equal matter, called pus, is generated in the wound, and this produces very happy effects. . . . Hence laudable pus is esteemed by Surgeons the best of signs."[4]

What Dr. Jones is calling good news is now known to be a sign of an infected wound. He goes on to speak of the fever that arises at the same time and how this is necessary to the patient's being healed. Given this level of medical knowledge, it is no wonder that soldiers dreaded being wounded in battle.

Another obvious fear for a wounded soldier was of not being able to escape the battlefield and being taken prisoner by the enemy. Yankee Doodle Ebenezer Fletcher found himself in this situation when he was taken prisoner by the British. He tells of having his rifle misfire and "before I had time to discharge it, I received a musket ball in the small of my back, and fell." He crawled to a hiding place but eventually was found after the battle and taken prisoner. He was happily surprised at the medical care he received. "The Doctors appeared to be very kind and faithful. They pulled several pieces of my clothes from the wound, which were forced in by the [musket] ball I received."[5] As we will see in some of the prisoner of war accounts in the next chapter, such medical care after being captured was an unusual occurrence.

As is inevitable in war, not all soldiers recovered from their wounds. Many died before ever even having the chance to be taken from the field to receive medical care. One of the most disturbing chores for the soldiers was that of burying the dead who were left on the field at the end of a battle. British soldier Thomas Anburey writes of being assigned this "as unpleasant a duty as can fall to the lot of an officer" after the battle at Freeman's Farm, near Saratoga, New York, in September 1777. He writes that even though he found it unpleasant, at least he "observed a little more decency than some parties had done, who left heads, legs, and arms above ground."[6]

One of the most
disturbing chores
for the soldiers was
that of burying the
dead who were left
on the field at the
end of a battle.

Among the British, the dead were buried in mass graves, only the officers having the distinction of being buried individually. It must have been a grueling task indeed.

The fallen Continental soldiers received no better treatment. One soldier tells of burying the dead after Kings Mountain: "We proceeded to bury the dead, but it was badly done. They were thrown into convenient piles and covered with old logs, the bark of old trees, and rocks, yet not so as to secure them from becoming a prey to the beasts of the forests, or the vultures of the air."[7]

Another soldier recalls camping by the side of the road while on a march, being "poisoned with the stink of some rebels, who had been buried about three weeks in such a slight manner that wagons have cut up parts of the half-corrupted carcasses."[8] For loved ones who had heard of the deaths of their soldier in battle, it must have been difficult when the memoirs and eyewitness accounts were published after the war and they learned of what may have happened to their own soldier. But this was the only way it could be done, in the hurry after battle, with the soldiers themselves exhausted and soon to be back on the march.

For some of the soldiers, especially the officers, death would bring more humane treatment and remembrance. The death in battle of Dr. Joseph Warren of Boston occasioned an outpouring of lament and memories. Abigail Adams wrote to her husband, John, away at the Continental Congress: "My bursting heart must find vent at my pen. I have just heard, that our dear friend, Dr. Warren, is no more, but fell gloriously fighting for his country; saying, better to die honorably in the field, than ignominiously hang upon the gallows. Great is our loss. He has distinguished himself in every engagement, by his courage and fortitude, by animating the soldiers, and leading them on by his own example."[9]

Dr. Warren was a public figure, one of the leading supporters of the cause of independence in Boston, and he died a hero in the battle for Breed's Hill in June 1775. The combination of Warren's being a public figure, his death defending his home city, and the heroics of the militia's stand against the trained British troops, caused much grief. About seventy Patriot soldiers perished in this early battle, and their deaths, too, received considerable attention.

As the war progressed, death became more of a way of life, much less noted on the public scene, although no less mourned by the families. The more typical mention of death came after the war, in petitions of widows and children of dead soldiers, who lost everything when their husbands or fathers died

Dr. Joseph Warren, a prominent citizen of Boston, was mourned widely upon his death early in the war. As the war dragged on, people became more accustomed to the deaths around them, and public mourning like that for Warren was less common.

in battle. Such is the case of a widow named Elizabeth Forbes whose militiaman husband was killed in the fighting at Guilford Courthouse in 1781. She petitioned the legislature: "I must trouble your Honourable Body with a small account of my distressed condition . . . Petitioner's Husband . . .

received a mortal wound of which he afterward died. And your Petitioner being left with a helpless family of Small children is at this time in great distress."[10] She was granted two years of tax relief for her loss.

Being wounded in battle and sometimes dying from the wounds received is, of course, part of war. What lingers over two hundred years after the Revolutionary War is the horror of what the wounded suffered and the losses felt by those they left behind. For some of these soldiers, who came from far across the ocean in Great Britain or Germany, their loved ones would never even see the land where they died—the soldiers would lie forever in some mass grave, as enemies buried in foreign soil. The soldiers who lived and knew that death might be their fate next, bravely and honorably continued their fight, whichever side they fought for in this conflict.

CHAPTER NINE

Prisoner of War

"Now we must go on bord of a new Ship and be put in irons & crouded Down betwixt Decks half starved like poor devils . . . in this languishing condition we were obliged to stay suffering all that those devils on earth (or rather Hell afloat) could inflict."[1] The prison ships of the British occasioned more horror among the soldiers than the risk of battle.

As complaints mounted of mistreatment of American soldiers taken prisoner by the British, General Washington appointed Elias Boudinot, who had been president of the Continental Congress, to visit the prisoners and study their situation. Washington contacted the British generals and made arrangements for Boudinot to be allowed access to the prisoners. The British commander, General James Robertson, welcomed Boudinot, but he was disappointed when Boudinot reported back that

conditions were even worse than he had heard. The British general blamed the misconduct on lower-ranking officers who were not following the common rules of war.

What Boudinot reported back to Washington were inexcusable violations of the proper treatment of prisoners—prisoners being "locked up in the Dungeon on the most trifling pretenses, such as asking for more water for drink on a hot day," a wounded soldier who was "put into the Dungeon & remained there 10 weeks totally forgotten by the General, and never had his wound dressed," prisoners fed with "4 lb hard spoiled Biscuit & 2 lb Pork per week; which they were obliged to Eat raw," and the officer in charge of the prison who had "come down and beat them unmercifully with a Rattan & Knock them down with his fist."[2] General Robertson promised to improve these conditions.

The prison ships of the British occasioned more horror among the soldiers than the risk of battle.

Prisoners taken in battles out in the countryside seemed to be treated better than those who had the misfortune to find themselves on the prison ships in New York City. One Yankee Doodle, Ebenezer Fletcher, observed what was probably true about all of those who held captives: "The difference in mankind never struck me more sensibly then while a prisoner. Some would do everything in their power to make me comfortable . . . others abused me with the vilest of language; telling me that the prisoners would all be hanged; that they would drive all the damned rebels into the sea." Fletcher accepted as natural that "I was stripped of everything valuable about me."[3]

Another Continental army officer, Captain Jabez Fitch, had similar words to say about his imprisonment: "Some . . . treated us with proper Respect, and others with mean and low lived Insolence Despizing & Rideculing the mean appearance of many of us who had been stripp'd and abused . . . nor did they forget to Remind us of the British Laws against Rebellion, Treason, etc., with many of their own learned Comments thereon, which seemed to give them wonderfull Consolation."[4]

One serious problem for those Americans taken prisoner on the frontier was their treatment by the natives who were allied with the British troops.

Many accounts support the following diary entry of one Continental soldier, Benjamin Stevens, who was taken prisoner in 1776 by "savages" who initially wanted just to kill their captives until British officers intervened, "promising them our plunder. Accordingly the savages strip'd them almost naked and delivered them up to the King's Troops. And the 21st next morning the savages came where we were and stript us of whatever pleased them, and so continued till they had got almost all we had."[5]

The question naturally arises of whether the British or Hessian soldiers taken prisoner were treated better than the Americans. One account would indicate that they were. A Hessian soldier, Dr. J. F. Wasmus, remembered being taken prisoner after the Battle of Saratoga. His personal things and medical equipment were taken, but when he complained, were returned to him. He found the quarters where they were held crowded, but he was pleased with how they were fed: "We got fresh beef this noon, which was put in big chunks in a trough placed upon the table together with Turkish wheat bread. . . . A vessel with water was placed in the room and each could drink as he pleased."[6]

Redcoat John Robert Shaw was taken prisoner and his uniform was stolen. He indignantly protested that no British officer would have allowed that to happen to an American prisoner but was forced to comply. He acknowledged, though, that his captives certainly seemed to need his clothes, "for such ragged mortals I never saw in my life before, to pass under the character of soldiers."[7]

Shaw acknowledges that "the treatment of the prisoners in general during the American war was harsh, severe, and in many instances, inhuman."[8] It is interesting to note that Shaw, while a prisoner of war, decided to change sides and ended the war serving with the Continental army.

The harsh treatment received by prisoners resulted in a high death rate among them, as can be seen in this report on prison conditions that appeared in an American newspaper:

In this situation, without clothes, without victuals or drink, and even water, . . . without fire, a number of them sick . . . for four months without blankets, bedding, or straw. . . . No wonder they all became sickly, and having at the same time no medicine, no help of physicians . . . died by scores in a night. . . . By these means . . . fifteen hundred brave Americans, who had nobly gone forth in defence of their injured, oppressed country, but whom the chance of war had cast into the hands of our enemies, died in New York.[9]

Little wonder then that the soldiers dreaded the very thought of becoming prisoners.

CHAPTER TEN

The Surrender at Yorktown

Lord Cornwallis cannot sufficiently express his gratitude to the Officers & Soldiers of the Army for their good conduct on any occasion since he has had the honor to command them, but particularly for their extraordinary Courage & perseverance in the defence of this Post, he sincerely laments that their efforts have not been successful, but the Powerfull Artillery which was opposed to them could not be resisted & the blood of the bravest men would have been shed in vain.[1]

With these words on October 19, 1781, Lord Cornwallis said his good-byes to his army.

Two days previously, the unthinkable had happened. Eight thousand British troops, one fourth of the entire British army in the colonies, had surrendered to the American and French forces. Although the war would not officially end until 1783, with this surrender the British effectively lost the war to maintain their hold on their former colony.

Events had been set in motion the previous month when a French fleet had defeated the British fleet in the Chesapeake Bay, leaving the British and Hessian troops on the peninsula stranded, without access to supplies or relief. Wrote James Thacher: "This event is of infinite importance, and fills our hearts with joy, as we can now proceed on our expedition." The expedition he referred to was George Washington's decision to move his Continental army down to Virginia by water. A fleet of "eighty vessels are in readiness, great activity prevails, embarkation has commenced and our horses are sent round to

General Lord Cornwallis bade his army good-bye on October 19, 1781, the day of the surrender at Yorktown, Virginia.

Virginia by land," wrote Dr. Thacher.[2] Joined by the French troops commanded by General Rochambeau, they would have a force that outnumbered the cutoff British army.

On the march on September 28 after the British army, Pennsylvanian William Feltman wrote in his diary: "I conjecture the whole of our army, I mean the French and our Continental troops, to be Fifteen Thousand Veteran Troops, besides the militia; they are so numerous that I have not been able to ascertain their number." He and a fellow soldier, Captain John Davis, were so sure of success coming quickly that they made a bet about how soon the British would be forced to surrender. Davis, the more opti-

mistic, "laid a bet with me of a beaver hat that Lord Cornwallis and his army would be prisoners of war by the next Sunday."[3]

The victory that the Continental soldiers felt in the air would take somewhat longer than that, but it was probably a sure thing to bet on by then. The American and French troops began a slow but steady attack on the British fortified position at Yorktown, moving ever closer as the days went by. Within their first set of lines, the combined armies built "a second parallel line, and batteries within about three hundred yards, this was effected in the night, and at day light the enemy were roused to the greatest exertions. . . . The siege is becoming more and more formidable and alarming," wrote Dr. Thacher.[4]

Deserters from the besieged fort were giving the Americans even more reason to be sure of success. Lieutenant Feltman recorded in his diary a conversation with one deserter: "He informed us that Cornwallis had given out orders to them not to be afraid of the Americans, that they had not any heavy pieces of ordinance except a few pieces of field artillery. He also informed the soldiery and inhabitants that the French fleet was inferior to him and were afraid to attack him. . . . Such are my Lord's addresses to his soldiery, but they have more sense than to believe his weak expressions."[5]

In fact, the American and French armies did have heavy artillery to use against the British, and they continued to pound away at their fortifications. Wrote Dr. Thacher:

Being in the trenches every other night and day, I have a fine opportunity of witnessing the sublime and stupendous scene. . . . The bomb shells from the besiegers and the besieged are incessantly crossing each other's path in the air. They are clearly visible in the form of a black ball in the day, but in the night, they appear like a fiery meteor with a blazing tail, most beautifully brilliant, ascending majestically from the mortar to a certain altitude, and gradually descending to the spot where they are destined to execute their work of destruction. . . . When a shell falls, it whirls around, burrows, and excavates the earth to a considerable extent, and bursting, makes dreadful havoc around. I have more than once witnessed fragments of the mangled bodies and limbs of the British soldiers, thrown in the air by the bursting of our shells.[6]

The situation became increasingly desperate for the soldiers inside the fort. Hessian soldier John Ewald wrote of the decision to send away the "black friends" (mostly slaves loaned to them by southern Loyalists) that they had used to "despoil the countryside" because they could no longer find enough food to feed them. There was also a problem finding food for their horses, but the horses could not just be sent away since they would be useful to the enemy. Ewald reported sadly that the animals "were killed and dragged into the York River."[7] As their ammunition and food ran low, Cornwallis began to run out of possible options for the soldiers also.

On the night of October 14, "two of our Regiments of Light Infantry, under the command of the Marquis de Lafayette, came to the trenches. Immediately after, they advanced towards the enemy's two out-works, which they stormed and carried with success with the loss of a few killed and wounded," wrote Continental soldier Feltman. The following day, the "Second Parallel line" was complete "within two hundred and fifty yards of the enemy's main works."[8]

On October 17, Cornwallis and Washington communicated back and forth by messenger as Cornwallis attempted to obtain the best terms he could get for surrendering his army. The surrender itself occurred two days later, on October 19, at three in the afternoon. Recorded Hessian Johann Prectel: "We marched through both armies and where they

"When a shell falls, it whirls around, burrows, and excavates the earth to a considerable extent, and bursting, makes dreadful havoc around."

ended, we marched in two lines and at four-forty-five lay down our weapons."[9] Fellow Hessian officer Johann Ewald called it "the melancholy parade."[10]

Feltman commented that "[t]he British prisoners all appeared to be much in liquor."[11] Cornwallis pleaded ill health and did not even attend the surrender ceremony. His second in command tried to surrender to the French commander rather than to General Washington, to ease the humiliation of the defeat. Wrote Dr. Thacher: "Every eye was prepared to gaze on Lord Cornwallis, the object of peculiar interest and solicitude; but he disappointed our anxious expectations; pretending indisposition, he made General O'Hara his substitute as leader."[12]

American Colonel Benjamin Tallmadge described the scene: "Never was mortification greater than this haughty, cruel, plundering army exhibited on this humiliating occasion. The joy and exultation were proportionately great in the allied army, although not the smallest insult was offered to the prisoners."[13]

Dr. Thacher also noted how well the Americans behaved at the surrender and that the British could not claim the same. "In their line of march we remarked a disorderly and unsoldierly conduct, their step was irregular, and their ranks frequently broken. But it was in the field, when they came to the last act of the drama, that the spirit and pride of the British soldier was put to the severest test: here their mortification could not be concealed . . . many of the soldiers manifested a *sullen temper,* throwing their arms on the pile with violence."[14]

As word of the surrender spread, there was great celebration throughout the nation. The *New Jersey Gazette* reported on October 28 that "yesterday the great and important event of the surrender of Lord Cornwallis and his whole army, to the combined forces commanded by his Excellency General Washington, was celebrated at Trenton . . . with every mark of joy and festivity. The day was ushered in with the beating of drums, and the American colors were displayed in various parts of the town. . . . At noon a proper discharge of cannon was fired. . . . At seven in the evening the company retired, and the rejoicings were concluded by a brilliant illumination."[15]

For the Continental soldiers, the greatest praise came from their commander in chief: "The General congratulates the army upon the glorious event of yesterday . . . to communicate his thanks to the officers and soldiers of their respective commands . . . for the great skill and alacrity with which they performed the several duties assigned them during the siege against York. He ever entertained the highest opinion of the troops, but the spirit and bravery which was so conspicuous on the present occasion has given him additional confidence in them and secured his warmest and lasting friendship."[16]

Although this lithograph is entitled "Surrender of Cornwallis at Yorktown, Virginia," the British officer surrendering the sword is General Charles O'Hara, since Cornwallis did not attend the surrender ceremony.

Amid celebration and fanfare, newly elected President Washington arrives in New York City in 1789 for his inauguration.

CHAPTER ELEVEN

Winners and Losers

On September 3, 1783, a peace treaty was signed, ending the Revolutionary War. In November of the same year, the last British troops left American soil when the British surrendered New York City.

The colonists had done the impossible—they had achieved their independence from the world's mightiest colonial power and the nation with the world's best army and navy. About 25,000 American soldiers had died to achieve this victory. The British had lost around 10,000 men and their Hessian allies another 7,500 or so. Countless other soldiers went home wounded or maimed or with illnesses that would plague them for their remaining years.

For the leaders of this revolution, victory would bring personal success. After several years of discussion and negotiation, a constitution would be approved in 1787. The first president elected would be the general who had pledged his honor to the cause and led the American armies throughout the conflict, George Washington. Two of the crafters of the Declaration of Independence and negotiators of the peace, John Adams and Thomas Jefferson, would follow him in that great office.

For the Loyalists, defeat meant that they felt unwelcome in this new country. About 14,000 of them left for Canada, the British colony that remained in the Americas. They settled in New Brunswick and tried to reestablish their lives with the monetary settlements they received for their lost goods and property from the United States government. Some moved to Great Britain. Others quietly remained in America and tried to reconstruct their lives and their relationships with their neighbors.

Many of the Hessian prisoners did not return home. About five thousand remained unaccounted

For the Loyalists, defeat meant that they felt unwelcome in this new country.

for at the end of the war. Historians speculate that these soldiers, fighting in a strange country for a king who was not theirs, defeated in battle and taken prisoner, quietly deserted while they were being marched through Pennsylvania and heard people (German immigrants to America) speaking their own language. Faced with an uncertain future, it was easier to disappear than to wait for the war to end and return home. Historians also document strong

support among the common Hessian soldiers for the fight for freedom going on in the colonies. Thus some of the desertions may have been for ideological as well as practical reasons.

These are the personal stories. How did the Revolution affect the world stage? The most immediate impact was on the French. Their revolution in 1789 would be sparked by both the ideals of the American Revolution and the fact that their country's treasury was empty because of all the money that had been spent supporting the American cause to defeat France's longtime enemy, Great Britain.

Great Britain had lost the war and had to accept the unbearable insult of welcoming the new ambassador of a power now her equal in the eyes of the world. Many of the issues between the former colonies and their mother country remained unresolved, and the two nations would meet again in battle a generation later in the War of 1812. Great Britain would try to reestablish her control, and even burn a portion of the capital of the new nation, but would ultimately be defeated. After that second war, the two nations would remain friends and allies for the future.

Within the new nation, some issues that should have been resolved with both the Declaration of Independence and the Constitution would continue to haunt the country for generations. The black soldiers who thought they were fighting for their own freedom would be disappointed by the decisions made by the new government. The divisions between the representatives of the northern industrial community and the southern slave-dependent plantation economy would only get worse with the passing of years. In 1861 the nation would divide again for a time in a Civil War, as the unresolved slavery issue and sectional conflicts tore the country apart for four long years.

For the Native Americans, the fact that so many tribes had supported Great Britain would only increase their sense of separation and lessen their chance of finding a place in this new society. The decision to grant land to soldiers as payment for their services in the Continental army sent people rushing to the frontiers, pushing the native peoples farther and farther into the interior. When the weakened French government sold their claims on the continent to President Jefferson in 1803, through the Louisiana Purchase, the new land stretched well beyond the Mississippi River. It would be only a matter of time before settlers would push even farther west to the Pacific Ocean, and the seemingly unlimited lands of the original settlers would be reduced to small reservations.

The ideals of freedom and independence would rock the world. At the surrender of Cornwallis's army at Yorktown, the defeated British army marched to the tune "The World Turned Upside Down," and indeed it had. It would take years, but the ultimate legacy of the American Revolution would not be just this new country that would become the world's greatest power. The legacy would also be the democratic fever that swept the world, destroying colonialism and establishing forever the belief that a country's citizens have a right to freedom and independence.

The Revolution Today

Even though the Revolutionary War ended well over two hundred years ago, it is still remembered by people who spend their free time reenacting the battles and camp life of that war. The reenactors are not just Patriots. Several Loyalists are remembered for their bravery fighting for the king. The Revolutionary War is also remembered at its many battlefield sites.

A visitor today can make the American Revolution come alive by traveling to places where these momentous events took place. You can walk across the bridge in Concord, Massachusetts, where the opening shots of the war were fired. There are battlefield parks at Saratoga, to commemorate the battle that determined that the colonists really could win the war; at Yorktown, where Cornwallis surrendered his army; at Cowpens and Kings Mountain in South Carolina; and at Morristown in New Jersey.

You can also relive the terrible winters at Mount Independence and Valley Forge.

A visitor can stand in the room in Independence Hall in Philadelphia where the Declaration of Independence was signed, or walk the streets of Boston on the Freedom Trail and be transported back to the days when that city led the colonies in rebellion. You can find information about your ancestors who fought in the Revolution. Descendants of these Patriots diligently research and document their lineages in order to become members of the Daughters or Sons of the American Revolution.

Even though the conflict ended so many years ago, the story of the war is still unfolding. Research still goes on as historians and archaeologists try to piece together an accurate picture of what happened in the war. In 1997 a Revolutionary War gunboat was found almost perfectly preserved in the cold waters of Lake Champlain by divers from the Lake Champlain Maritime Museum. Extensive research by historians finally confirmed three years later that the boat was the last of Benedict Arnold's gunboats, the *Spitfire,* a very special artifact of the Revolutionary War.

The story of the birth of this country—of these men and women of honor who risked their lives to bring to life the ideals of freedom—still holds the imagination not only of Americans but of people who come from around the world to visit the country that defied the world's greatest colonial power and won.

Revolutionary War reenactors help keep history alive by portraying soldiers and officers, both British and American, and faithfully re-creating the battles. These reenactors, dressed as British soldiers, march near Concord, Massachusetts.

SOURCE NOTES

PROLOGUE

1. Letter of George Washington, Philadelphia, June 18, 1775, a copy made from the original in 1849. Contained in *The Henley Smith Collection (Folder 2, Item #1397)*, Manuscript Division, Library of Congress.
2. Frederick Butler, *Memoirs of the Marquis De LaFayette* (Wethersfield, CT: Deming & Francis, 1825), p. 26.
3. William L. Stone, trans., *Memoirs and Letters and Journals of Major General Riedesel* (Albany: J. Munsell, 1868), p. 30.
4. Thomas Anburey, *With Burgoyne From Quebec* (Toronto: Macmillan of Canada, 1963), p. 176.
5. Lorenzo Sabine, *Biographical Sketches of Loyalists of the American Revolution, Vol. 1* (Boston: Little, Brown & Company, 1864), p. 207.

CHAPTER 1

1. *A Collection of Interesting, Authentic Papers, Relative to the Dispute Between Great Britain and America* (London: J. Almon, 1777), p. 7.
2. Jonathan Boucher, *Reminiscences of an American Loyalist 1783–1789* (Boston: Houghton Mifflin Company, 1925), p. 93.
3. Frank Moore, *Diary of the American Revolution From Newspapers and Original Documents, Vol. I* (New York: Charles Scribner, 1860), p. 25.

4. Eliza Yonge Wilkinson, *Letters of Eliza Wilkinson, During the Invasion and Possession of Charleston, S. C., by the British in the Revolutionary War* (New York: S. Colman, 1839), pp. 65–66.

CHAPTER 2

1. Frank Moore, *Diary of the American Revolution From Newspapers and Original Documents, Vol. I* (New York: Charles Scribner, 1860), p. 60.
2. Elias Boudinot, *Journal or Historical Recollections of American Events During the Revolutionary War* (Philadelphia: Frederick Bourquin, 1894), p. 1.
3. Winslow C. Watson, ed., *Men and Times of the Revolution; or, Memoirs of Elkanah Watson* (New York: Dana and Company, 1856), pp. 22–23.
4. Justin Kaplan, ed., *Bartlett's Familiar Quotations, Sixteenth Edition* (Boston: Little, Brown and Company, 1992), p. 310.
5. Letter of George Washington, Philadelphia, June 18, 1775, a copy made from the original in 1849. Contained in *The Henley Smith Collection (Folder 2, Item #1397)*, Manuscript Division, Library of Congress.
6. *Papers of John Hancock (Record Book No. 2, p. 4)*, Manuscript Division, Library of Congress.
7. John Shy, ed., *Winding Down: The Revolutionary War Letters*

of Lieutenant Benjamin Gilbert of Massachusetts, 1780–1783 (Ann Arbor: University of Michigan Press, 1989), p. 25.

8. James Thacher, *A Military Journal During the American Revolutionary War, From 1775 to 1783* (Boston: Richardson and Lord, 1823), pp. 71–72.

9. *Orderly Book of the Northern Army at Ticonderoga and Mt. Independence, From October 17th, 1776, to January 8th, 1777* (Albany: J. Munsell, 1859), p. 24.

10. Elizabeth Evans, *Weathering the Storm: Women of the American Revolution* (New York: Charles Scribner's Sons, 1975), p. 10.

11. Herman Mann, *The Female Review: or, Memoirs of an American Young Lady* (Dedham, MA: Nathaniel and Benjamin Heaton, 1797), p. 169.

12. Sidney Kaplan, *The Black Presence in the Era of the American Revolution 1770–1800* (Washington, D.C.: The Smithsonian Institution, 1973), p. 36.

13. Thomas S. Abler, ed., *Chainbreaker: The Revolutionary War Memoirs of Governor Blacksnake* (Lincoln: University of Nebraska Press, 1989), p. 50.

14. Colin G. Calloway, *The American Revolution in Indian Country* (Cambridge: Cambridge University Press, 1995), p. 26.

15. Wallace Brown, *The Good Americans: The Loyalists in the American Revolution* (New York: William Morrow and Company, Inc., 1969), pp. 115, 117.

CHAPTER 3

1. Frank Moore, *Diary of the American Revolution From Newspapers and Original Documents, Vol. I* (New York: Charles Scribner, 1860), p. 61.

2. Marion Balderston and David Syrett, eds., *The Lost War: Letters from British Officers During the American Revolution* (New York: Horizon Press, 1975), pp. 81, 147.

3. *The Henley Smith Papers (Folder 2, Item #1413)*, Manuscript Division, Library of Congress.

4. Thomas Anburey, *With Burgoyne from Quebec* (Toronto: Macmillan of Canada, 1963), p. 175.

5. Wallace Brown, *The Good Americans: The Loyalists in the American Revolution* (New York: William Morrow and Company, Inc., 1969), p. 113.

6. Ray W. Pettengill, trans., *Letters From America 1776–1779* (Port Washington, NY: Kennikat Press, 1924), p. xx.

7. William L. Stone, trans., *Memoirs and Letters and Journals of Major General Riedesel* (Albany: J. Munsell, 1868), p. 238.

8. Stone, p. 237.

9. Stone, pp. 234, 236.

10. John P. Becker, *The Sexagenary; or Reminiscences of the American Revolution* (Albany, NY: J. Munsell, 1866), pp. 120–121.

11. Edward E. Hale, *Franklin in France* (Boston: Roberts Brothers, 1888), pp. 63–64.

12. Frederick Butler, *Memoirs of the Marquis De LaFayette* (Wethersfield, CT: Deming & Francis, 1825), p. 27.

13. M.W.E. Wright, trans., *Memoirs of the Marshal Count de Rochambeau, Relative to the War of Independence of the United States* (Paris: French, English, and American Library, 1838), pp. 22–23, 69.

14. Joseph P. Tustin, trans., *Diary of the American War: A Hessian Journal, Captain Johann Ewald* (New Haven: Yale University Press, 1979), p. 339.

CHAPTER 4

1. George F. Scheer and Hugh F. Rankin, *Rebels and Redcoats* (Cleveland: World Publishing Company, 1957), p. 289.

2. Joseph P. Tustin, trans., *Diary of the American War: A Hessian Journal, Captain Johann Ewald* (New Haven: Yale University Press, 1979), p. 55.

3. Ray W. Pettengill, trans., *Letters From America 1776–1779* (Port Washington, NY: Kennikat Press, 1924), p. 99.

4. James Thacher, *A Military Journal During the American*

Revolutionary War, From 1775 to 1783 (Boston: Richardson and Lord, 1823), p. 153.

5. Ebenezer Huntington, *Letters Written by Ebenezer Huntington During the American Revolution* (New York: Chas. Fred. Heartman, 1914), pp. 80–81.

6. John Laurens, *The Army Correspondence of Colonel John Laurens in the Years 1777–8* (New York: The Bradford Club, 1867), p. 126.

7. *Papers of John Hancock (Record Book No. 2, pp. 116–117),* Manuscript Division, Library of Congress.

8. *Orderly Book of Capt. Ichabod Norton of Col. Mott's Regiment* (Fort Edward, NY: Keating & Barnard, 1898), p. 14.

9. Frank Moore, *Diary of the American Revolution From Newspapers and Original Documents, Vol. I* (New York: Charles Scribner, 1860), p. 445.

10. *Orderly Book of Capt. Ichabod Norton,* p. 26.

11. William L. Stone, trans., *Memoirs and Letters and Journals of Major General Riedesel* (Albany: J. Munsell, 1868), p. 235.

12. Entry for February 22, 1778, *Valley Forge Orderly Book, 1778.* Manuscript Division, Library of Congress.

13. Helga Doblin, trans., *An Eyewitness Account of the American Revolution and New England Life: The Journal of J. F. Wasmus, German Company Surgeon, 1776–1783* (New York: Greenwood Press, 1990), p. 27.

14. Herbert T. Wade and Robert A. Lively, *This Glorious Cause . . . The Adventures of Two Company Officers in Washington's Army* (Princeton: Princeton University Press, 1958), pp. 54, 212.

15. Walter Hart Blumenthal, *Women Camp Followers of the American Revolution* (New York: Arno Press, 1974), pp. 93, 42.

16. Blumenthal, p. 64.

17. Thacher, pp. 189–190.

18. C. Keith Wilbur, *The Revolutionary Soldier 1775–1783* (Guilford, CT: The Globe Pequot Press, 1993), p. 67.

CHAPTER 5

1. Frederic R. Kirkland, ed., *Journal of Lewis Beebe* (Philadelphia: Historical Society of Philadelphia, 1935), p. 22.

2. Johann David Schoepff, *The Climate and Diseases of America* (Boston: H. O. Houghton, 1875), p. 22.

3. Richard L. Blanco, *Physician of the American Revolution, Jonathan Potts* (New York: Garland STPM Press, 1979), pp. 38–39.

4. Schoepff, p. 12.

5. James Thacher, *A Military Journal During the American Revolutionary War, From 1775 to 1783* (Boston: Richardson and Lord, 1823), p. 40.

6. Bayze Wells, *Journal of Bayze Wells* (Hartford: Connecticut Historical Society Collections, Vol. 7, 1899, pp. 241–296), p. 267.

7. Isaac Senter, *The Journal of Isaac Senter* (Philadelphia: Historical Society of Pennsylvania, 1846), p. 11.

CHAPTER 6

1. John Shy, ed., *Winding Down: The Revolutionary War Letters of Lieutenant Benjamin Gilbert of Massachusetts, 1780–1783* (Ann Arbor: University of Michigan Press, 1989), p. 45.

2. Elizabeth Cometti, ed., *The American Journals of Lt. John Enys* (Blue Mountain Lake, NY: Adirondack Museum, 1976), p. 42.

3. Joseph Plumb Martin, *Private Yankee Doodle* (Boston: Little, Brown and Company, 1962), p. 98.

4. Isaac Senter, *The Journal of Isaac Senter* (Philadelphia: Historical Society of Pennsylvania, 1846), p. 5.

5. Senter, p. 6.

6. Ray W. Pettengill, trans., *Letters From America 1776–1779* (Port Washington, NY: Kennikat Press, 1924), p. 121.

7. Thomas Hughes, *A Journal by Thos. Hughes for his Amusement, & Designed only for his Perusal by the Time He*

Attains the Age of 50 if He Lives So Long (Cambridge: Cambridge University Press, 1947), p. 8.

8. William L. Stone, trans., *Memoirs and Letters and Journals of Major General Riedesel* (Albany: J. Munsell, 1868), p. 234.

CHAPTER 7

1. Benjamin Tallmadge, *Memoir of Col. Benjamin Tallmadge* (New York: Thomas Holman, 1858), pp. 9–10.
2. W.T.R. Saffell, *Records of the Revolutionary War Containing the Military and Financial Correspondence of Distinguished Officers* (New York: Pudney & Russell, Publishers, 1858), p. 342.
3. Elias Boudinot, *Journal or Historical Recollections of American Events During the Revolutionary War* (Philadelphia: Frederick Bourquin, 1894), p. 1.
4. *The Military Journals of Two Private Soldiers, 1758–1775* (Poughkeepsie, NY: Abraham Tomlinson, 1855), p. 51.
5. Abigail Adams, *Letters of Mrs. Adams, the wife of John Adams* (Boston: Wilkins, Carter, and Co., 1848), p. 35.
6. Isaac Senter, *The Journal of Isaac Senter* (Philadelphia: Historical Society of Pennsylvania, 1846), pp. 37–39.
7. John C. Dann, *The Revolution Remembered: Eyewitness Accounts of the War for Independence* (Chicago: The University of Chicago Press, 1980), p. 175.
8. Edward Bangs, ed., *Journal of Lieutenant Isaac Bangs, April 1 to July 29, 1776* (Cambridge: John Wilson and Son, 1890), p. 11.
9. Marion Balderston and David Syrett, eds., *The Lost War: Letters From British Officers During the American Revolution* (New York: Horizon Press, 1975), p. 77.
10. Persifer Frazer, "Letters From Ticonderoga," *Bulletin of the Fort Ticonderoga Museum, Vol. X, No. 6, January 1962)*, pp. 455–456.
11. Thomas Hughes, *A Journal by Thos. Hughes for his Amusement, & Designed only for his Perusal by the Time He*

Attains the Age of 50 if He Lives So Long (Cambridge: Cambridge University Press, 1947), p. 6.

12. Tallmadge, p. 9.
13. William Jennison, *Diary of William Jennison*, Manuscript Division, Library of Congress, entry of October 28, 1776.
14. Enoch Anderson, *Personal Recollections of Captain Enoch Anderson* (Wilmington: Historical Society of Delaware, 1896), p. 28.
15. Anderson, p. 29.
16. James Thacher, *A Military Journal During the American Revolutionary War, From 1775 to 1783* (Boston: Richardson and Lord, 1823), p. 85.
17. Thacher, pp. 127–128.
18. Ray W. Pettengill, trans., *Letters From America 1776–1779* (Port Washington, NY: Kennikat Press, 1924), pp. 102–105.
19. Thacher, pp. 116–117.
20. Friederika Charlotte de Riedesel, *Letters and Memoirs Relating to the War of American Independence* (New York: G. & C. Carvill, 1827), pp. 187–188.
21. Robert Bray and Paul E. Bushnell, eds., *Diary of a Common Soldier in the American Revolution, 1775–1783* (DeKalb: Northern Illinois University Press, 1978), p. 122.
22. Lloyd A. Brown and Howard H. Peckham, eds., *Revolutionary War Journals of Henry Dearborn 1775–1783* (Freeport, NY: Books for Libraries Press, 1939), p. 128.
23. Thacher, p. 201.
24. Thacher, p. 251.
25. R. Ernest Dupuy and Trevor N. Dupuy, *An Outline History of the American Revolution* (New York: Harper & Row, Publishers, 1975), p. 164.
26. Thacher, p. 305.

CHAPTER 8

1. Hugh F. Rankin, *The American Revolution* (New York: Capricorn Books, 1964), p. 262.

2. John Jones, *Plain Concise Practical Remarks on the Treatment of Wounds and Fractures* (Philadelphia: Robert Bell, 1776), p. 12.

3. Jones, p. 14.

4. Jones, p. 16.

5. Ebenezer Fletcher, *Narrative of the Captivity & Sufferings of Ebenezer Fletcher* (New Ipswich, NH: S. Wilder, 1827), pp. 12, 15.

6. Thomas Anburey, *With Burgoyne from Quebec* (Toronto: Macmillan of Canada, 1963), p. 176.

7. James Potter Collins, *Autobiography of a Revolutionary Soldier* (Clinton, LA: Feliciana Democrat, 1859), pp. 6–7.

8. Richard M. Dorson, *America Rebels* (New York: Pantheon, 1953), p. 129.

9. Abigail Adams, *Letters of Mrs. Adams, the wife of John Adams* (Boston: Wilkins, Carter, and Co., 1848), p. 31.

10. Cynthia A. Kierner, *Southern Women in Revolution, 1776–1800* (Columbia: University of South Carolina Press, 1998), p. 31.

CHAPTER 9

1. Miriam and Wes Herwig, eds., *Jonathan Carpenter's Journal* (Randolph Center, VT: Greenhills Books, 1994), p. 48.

2. Elias Boudinot, *Journal or Historical Recollections of American Events During the Revolutionary War* (Philadelphia: Frederick Bourquin, 1894), pp. 15, 17–18.

3. Ebenezer Fletcher, *Narrative of the Captivity & Sufferings of Ebenezer Fletcher* (New Ipswich, NH: S. Wilder, 1827), pp. 18–19.

4. Jabez Fitch, *Diary of Captain Jabez Fitch* (privately published by Vernon D. Fitch, Hyde Park, VT, 1899), unpaged.

5. Benjamin Stevens, *Journal of Benjamin Stevens.* Manuscript Division, Library of Congress, p. 9.

6. Helga Doblin, trans., *An Eyewitness Account of the American Revolution and New England Life: The Journal of J. F. Wasmus, German Company Surgeon, 1776–1783* (New York: Greenwood Press, 1990), p. 74.

7. John Robert Shaw, *An Autobiography of Thirty Years, 1777–1807* (Athens: Ohio University Press, 1992), p. 42.

8. Shaw, p. 47.

9. Frank Moore, *Diary of the American Revolution From Newspapers and Original Documents, Vol. I* (New York: Charles Scribner, 1860), p. 377.

CHAPTER 10

1. *Orderly Book of the British Army, May 23–Oct. 22, 1781.* Manuscript Division, Library of Congress.

2. James Thacher, *A Military Journal During the American Revolutionary War, From 1775 to 1783* (Boston: Richardson and Lord, 1823), pp. 332, 329.

3. William Feltman, *The Journal of Lieut. William Feltman, of the First Pennsylvania Regiment, 1781–82* (Philadelphia: Historical Society of Pennsylvania, 1853), pp. 15, 16.

4. Thacher, p. 340.

5. Feltman, p. 18.

6. Thacher, pp. 340–341.

7. Joseph P. Tustin, trans., *Diary of the American War: A Hessian Journal, Captain Johann Ewald* (New Haven: Yale University Press, 1979), pp. 335–336.

8. Feltman, pp. 20–21.

9. Johann Ernst Prechtel, *A Hessian Officer's Diary of the American Revolution* (Bowie, MD: Heritage Books, Inc., 1994), p. 88.

10. Tustin, p. 339.

11. Feltman, p. 22.

12. Thacher, p. 346.

13. Benjamin Tallmadge, *Memoir of Col. Benjamin Tallmadge* (New York: Thomas Holman, 1858), p. 45.

14. Thacher, p. 347.

15. Frank Moore, *Diary of the American Revolution From Newspapers and Original Documents, Vol. II* (New York: Charles Scribner, 1860), pp. 519–521.

16. Feltman, pp. 22–23.

A Brief Chronology of the Revolutionary War

April 19, 1775	Battle of Lexington and Concord
June 17, 1775	Battle of Bunker Hill
March 1776	Evacuation of Boston by the British
July 4, 1776	Declaration of Independence signed
July 1776	British begin occupation of New York City
October 11–12, 1776	Battle of Valcour Island
December 26, 1776	Battle of Trenton
September 1777	British begin occupation of Philadelphia
October 7, 1777	Battle of Saratoga
June 1778	British evacuate Philadelphia
June 28, 1778	Battle of Monmouth Court House
July 15–16, 1779	Battle of Stony Point
September 1779	Battle of Savannah
April 1780	Battle of Charleston
October 7, 1780	Battle of Kings Mountain
March 15, 1781	Battle of Guilford Courthouse
September 28–October 19, 1781	Battle of Yorktown British surrender one fourth of their troops in America
November 18, 1781	British evacuate Wilmington, North Carolina
July 11, 1782	British evacuate Savannah, Georgia
December 14, 1782	British evacuate Charleston, South Carolina
September 3, 1783	Peace treaty signed between British and Americans
November 25, 1783	Last British troops on American soil begin evacuation of New York City and Long Island

For Further Information

BOOKS

Adler, Jeanne Winston. *In the Path of War: Children of the American Revolution Tell Their Stories.* Peterborough, NH: Cobblestone Publishing Company, 1998.

Beller, Susan Provost. *Revolutionary War (Letters From the Home Front).* Tarrytown, NY: Benchmark Books, 2001.

Bliven, Bruce. *The American Revolution.* New York: Random House, 1987.

Dolan, Edward F. *The American Revolution: How We Fought the War of Independence.* Brookfield, CT: Millbrook Press, 1995.

Egger-Bovet, Howard. *Book of the American Revolution.* Boston: Little, Brown & Company, 1994.

Gay, Kathlyn. *Revolutionary War: Voices from the Past.* Brookfield, CT: Twenty-First Century Books, 1995.

Grant, Rich. G. *The American Revolution (Revolution!).* Stamford, CT: Thomson Learning, 1995.

Kent, Deborah. *The American Revolution: "Give Me Liberty, or Give Me Death."* Springfield, NJ: Enslow Publishers, 1994.

Marrin, Albert. *The War for Independence: The Story of the American Revolution.* New York: Atheneum, 1988.

Massof, Joy. *American Revolution, 1700–1800.* New York: Scholastic Press, 2000.

Meyeroff, Stephen. *The Call for Independence: The Story of the American Revolution and Its Cause.* Claremont, CA: Oak Tree Publishing, 1996.

Moore, Kay. *If You Lived at the Time of the American Revolution.* New York: Scholastic Press, 1998.

Murphy, Jim. *A Young Patriot: The American Revolution as Experienced by One Boy.* Boston: Houghton Mifflin Company, 1996.

Steins, Richard. *A Nation Is Born.* Brookfield, CT: Twenty-First Century Books, 1993.

Weber, Michael. *The American Revolution.* Chatham, NJ: Raintree/Steck Vaughn, 2000.

PLACES TO VISIT

Boston National Historical Park (Massachusetts)

Colonial National Historical Park (includes Yorktown battlefield, Virginia)

Cowpens National Battlefield (South Carolina)

Guilford Courthouse National Military Park (North Carolina)

Independence National Historical Park (Philadelphia, Pennsylvania)

Kings Mountain National Military Park (South Carolina)

Minute Man National Historical Park (includes Lexington and Concord, Massachusetts)

Moores Creek National Battlefield (South Carolina)
Morristown National Historical Park (New Jersey)
Saratoga National Historical Park (New York)
Valley Forge National Historical Park (Pennsylvania)

All of these sites can be accessed from the National Parks Service at www.nps.gov

Others:
Fort Ticonderoga (New York)
    www.fort-ticonderoga.org
Mount Independence Historic Site (Vermont)
    www.state.vt.us/dca/historic/mt_indy.htm

VIDEOS
American Revolution (PBS Documentary)
The Crossing (A&E)

ALSO ON THE INTERNET
Archiving Early America: Historic Documents from 18th–Century America
www.earlyamerica.com
Great source for pamphlets, speeches, and other primary source material for colonial America and the Revolutionary War.

Liberty! The American Revolution: Chronicle of the Revolution
www.pbs.org/ktca/liberty/chronicle
Excellent topical coverage of all aspects of the Revolutionary War, including battles, political events, and the lives of the common people of the time.

National Archives and Records Administration: Online Exhibit Hall
www.nara.gov
See original copies of the Declaration of Independence and the U.S. Constitution. This site also links to NAIL, the National Archives site with copies of materials from their collections.

Special Collections in the Library of Congress: Eighteenth Century
lcweb.loc.gov/spcoll/clist18.html
Descriptions of materials available through the Library of Congress on the Revolutionary War and the colonial period.

Spy Letters of the American Revolution, Clements Library, University of Michigan
www.si.umich.edu/SPIES/index.html
Digital reproductions of actual letters from the Revolutionary War period with transcriptions and context information.

Index